GW00750442

Carolann's Progression

The Gateway to Understanding Your Life's Ultimate Journey

Carolann Frankie and
Roland Bush-Cavell

Published by Mind Body Soul Development Organisation
Limited

For more information on our work, please visit
www.carolannspathway.co.uk or email
info@carolannspathway.co.uk

ISBN 978-0-9576596-3-6

Contents

Disclaimer

This book is written with the purpose of conveying the author's perceptions of a spiritual universe which, it is our belief, can be accessed by all those who wish to do so. It is not therefore our intention to prove anything to you, rather we offer here our perspective on a pathway that we sincerely wish may offer you insight.

Please remember that what might work for one person may not necessarily work for another and while we offer meditations on healing and discuss how to channel energies, nothing within this book is offered for diagnosis, prescription or treatment of any health disorder whatsoever. You should consult a medical practitioner for any complaint or medical condition, either diagnosed or suspected and no element of this book is intended to replace the advice of a competent healthcare professional. Faith, be it those of the authors, or your own can only be gained through personal experience and choice. It is your prerogative to believe as you wish, be it the nature of the beginnings of life on Earth, what pathway you follow, whether you recognise God, and if you do, by what name you call Him.

Introduction

In Carolann's Pathway we sought to enlighten you to the world that exists beyond our Earthly plane, while providing tools for your spiritual and psychic development.

Here, in Carolann's Progression, we seek to introduce a pathway to greater self-knowledge and awareness, channelled from the spiritual realms, that provides a route to understanding that which is currently unknown to us, both within and without.

Life follows the universal plan, with God as the Originator and, between the highest reaches of Heaven and our physical reality are realms of existence, created by Him, where our souls and all spiritual beings belong. This book is concerned with understanding the two worlds, the nature of their union and the role each plays with the other. We seek to bring the wisdom of the 'spirit world' here, so that those who dwell there might awaken us to its presence and help us understand the true nature and ultimate purpose of our physical existence.

Life is a cleansing process and for many of us at this time there is a vast distance, a huge gap, between Heaven and Earth. Much of the human race sees bridging the gap between these two worlds as an unattainable ambition, if they recognise this 'other' spiritual world at all and yet this seemingly impossible task is, in reality, not difficult.

Heaven, and the potential to attain it, is all around us and there are many ways we can awaken to its presence. Seeking to be in-tune with oneself and treading a pathway of self-understanding helps open a doorway to the spiritual side of life. If we open ourselves and allow the possibility that there is more to life than we currently understand; that a spiritual dimension may exist, then our minds are already prepared to expand. If we accept the presence of the spiritual, then we are able to work with it, paving the way to improve our communication with the inner-self, sensing spiritual energy and stretching our minds. By walking this pathway we can learn to comprehend the realms which exist outside of the physical and the role each level of our existence plays within life itself.

There are many stages, or levels, of spiritual development and each lifetime provides opportunities for us to learn, to step forwards and grow. So, each time we are born into a new physical body is an opportunity for us to progress to the next level on our journey. Our actions create consequences; we experience feelings of satisfaction, fear, dislike, love and exhilaration, depending not only upon what we face, but also the pathway we have chosen to follow and how we have previously reacted along the way.

The reason we are here is to experience the sensations of physical existence, to fully comprehend the consequences of our behaviour and appreciate every element of our being alive. For each life educates our soul, feeds it with the sensations of Earthly experience, gives it an opportunity to be aware, to appreciate which direction, thoughts and feelings are beneficial to its growth and to enable it to choose its pathway. By choosing the right course and becoming one with our soul, each of us can hope to have a permanent spiritual existence in spirit world and eventually in the highest level of all, in what we feel to be our Heaven.

Chapter One - A Spiritual Perspective

We may live many physical lives, hundreds and potentially thousands, each of which inform our soul through experience and aid our spiritual development. Each life is unique and may be short or long, beautiful, pleasant or painful, a source of despair or a cause for fulfilment. In each we can find love, opportunities to help others, loyalty and friendship and learn their value.

Even that which is painful to us serves a purpose, yet what may seem like our hardest lessons provide our greatest teaching and can instruct us in finding a positive direction. Challenges allow us to better know ourselves. Loss, hardship, loneliness and having to face our fears show us the negative side of life, the effects of actions, the results of what others do to us and the emptiness we may feel inside when we are starved of love. If we have suffered, then our pain provides contrast, so we might know that by embracing love, we can find the greatest joy. In our times of deepest need, it is those who love us and that which we are able to love, that provide not only comfort but a clue to life's ultimate purpose. For love can conquer all.

Yet no matter how diverse our experiences, a whole lifetime and even centuries of living throughout countless lives are fleeting when looked at from a spiritual perspective. The lessons we learn in this life may be chosen for us and as we elevate our conscious spiritual awareness that we gain an increasing independence in what journey we next take. Ultimately, we can choose whether we take another journey on the Earth plane or remain in spirit world. Yet, whatever situation we find ourselves in there are countless spiritual beings on the other side, alongside the souls of our loved ones, that wish to help us in our journey.

Like a mirror image in which everything is reversed, in spirit world we learn and grow spiritually, just as in the physical world we learn and grow physically. Our progression in spirit world reflects what we have learned from physical life. Our progression in the physical world reflects the day-to-day choices we make, the effort we expend and the good fortune we experience along the way. The shape of our lives and the influences we experience are all indications of the direction chosen for our journey and the lessons we may learn to further our spiritual development are presented along the way. So, if we are put on the planet to learn patience, we might find ourselves in stressful situations where things do not go the way we wish when we want them to. If, as a result, we learn fortitude and tolerance, we are acting positively and maturing spiritually.

In the same way that a baby is born from its mother into the physical world, so a soul is born into the spiritual world from God. Therefore, the soul is an extension of God's Creation and in His realm everything is spiritual. Unfettered by the needs of physical life, as pure soul energy we have no need of our physical senses and we need experience only the bliss which is a natural part of God's Creation. There we dwell in a non-physical, perfect place, where what we wish for is achieved through thought. Yet this spiritual existence does not stretch us, nor does it provide any of the experiences we gain from a physical life. So, in order to learn, we choose to be born into a physical body and experience worldly things through the senses of hearing, touch, taste, sight and smell. A physical existence also helps us to express our thoughts and manifest our wishes. Then, in turn, we bring this knowledge into our soul when we pass over, so that each life helps us to grow spiritually. This process of learning takes time and patience and may last many lifetimes. Just as a child will learn through familiarity, to understand exhilaration, joy, love, sadness and all the myriad emotions, we must first experience them on Earth. When each physical life ends, we take the essence of that life back with us and every lesson we learn expands our soul, feeding it with experiences through which it grows. As our soul expands through this Earthly input, we become more self-aware and as we gradually awaken to ourselves, recognise on an increasing number of levels the part we play in existence.

When a young soul is first born into a physical existence, united in the womb with a body, it is taking the first step on the road to testing its spiritual feelings of compassion, love and understanding in a physical environment; a true test of its spiritual nature. Before being born into the physical body, the soul will have existed spiritually, a consciousness that will have discovered up to a point, what direction of learning it wishes to take. Then, using the body as a vehicle, the soul can test how genuine to itself it is able to be. Just as in life, we may have many thoughts that we do not act upon or do not yet feel able to, so the soul may have emotions and ideas, aspirations as to what it can achieve that it requires a physical body to realise, to test how it might embody those aspirations. As a result, life is the process through which the soul will learn just how much of its spiritual being it is capable of bringing into reality, how much of itself it can realise in a worldly life.

Prior to its first life on Earth, our soul will have had no experience of the essence of physical life and of love. With no understanding of this concept, it will need to find and test all of those boundaries on Earth. Up until this point, the soul will know love only spiritually, as the very essence in which it dwells. Physical life makes it real, bringing us into contact with one another to live with love and its consequences. With this opportunity to care for and cherish one another comes the possibility of gaining and losing, of experiencing passion and physical consummation and of placing others first so that we may experience real joy.

Like a new-born baby, what a young soul experiences in its first lives on Earth is very important to its formative development. Therefore, the more examples of love, trust, integrity, responsibility and honesty a young soul is given, the more opportunities it has to recognise the value of such positive traits and the chance to build a physical life on strong foundations.

11

As our soul grows from immaturity into a more realised state, it will gain in knowledge and, if it learns positively, it will gain in wisdom. Therefore, older souls; those who have matured, can fulfil a purpose, not only of learning for themselves but also providing examples and guiding those who warrant a helping hand. How we act and how we communicate, if we choose to be a positive force in the world, will not only help those around us, it can also aid our spiritual growth. People who are recognised for their inner wisdom may be followed as examples, or consulted for advice. Following a spiritual pathway also aids our development so that when we are in our spiritual form between lives, we will find it easier to communicate with the living. By taking responsibility, we can lead by example and, in turn, help others to recognise the benefit of taking responsibility for their own actions. So, older souls can help those around them through the mere act of being.

We may not want to live in a world where there is the potential for both good and bad, positive and negative for fear of experiencing too much of the latter. Yet the fact that we are accountable for our actions, that they all produce a consequence, enables us to recognise the effects of what we do. As a result, we can choose a beneficial direction for our soul; we can make a choice to progress and follow our inner wisdom rather than be led by fear or negativity.

Without freedom of choice, the world would need to exist somehow devoid of consequences and would lack reality, for without consequences there would be little point to life.

Yet, despite the fact that we know positive from negative, right from wrong, good from bad, many of us choose to do bad things, things we know we would not like done to us. There are those who are malicious or merely act without regard for the feelings of others, those who are disruptive, or so negative about life that their limited viewpoint puts nothing positive into the world, or those who feel justified in acting negatively because they feel they have just cause - any of these can create irrevocable harm to ourselves and others.

Ultimately, these negative approaches are born out of ignorance, for if we recognised our role in the spiritual aspect of life, we would not harm one another. However, bad examples set by others do provide us with lessons so that we may establish right from wrong and choose what we wish to do with our own lives. So ignorance will not excuse us from the consequences of our actions, but by understanding we can ensure that we ourselves do not act in the same negative ways. For without victims we could not help those who are suffering, understand the effects of harming one another and taking the wrong direction, nor grow from the learning process.

Our soul is new when it is created in God's world, just as each body we occupy is new when it is created here. Each physical lifetime is a union, the creation of a physical form through which our soul may learn. When our soul first visits into the human race in this way, it can feel quite vulnerable and sometimes lost. It may take time to live in harmony with mankind, but our soul is never without connection to the Father in Heaven. Just as a human child benefits by bonding with its parents, so we may all benefit by allowing the spiritual connection with our Creator into our lives.

The soul may be progressed enough to make a distinct choice as to its purpose in life, or may be placed with divine guidance in a situation where certain types of lesson present themselves during its time on Earth. Therefore there is a purpose behind where we are born and to whom.

Inevitably, the process of learning our lessons can seem hard and life will naturally include challenges. Yet, however these lessons are learned, each soul can benefit from its experience of living with its fellow man.

The ultimate purpose of our physical existence is to fulfil the spiritual needs of our soul, because it is this innermost part of us which endures life after life and is the anchor that gives humanity its meaning. Bodily existence provides the soul with the joy of direct physical involvement and a structure through which we can experience the world. Being alive means we can create, reproduce, touch and sense and offers the opportunity to feel harmony and love. Alongside the good that life can bring, even negative experiences and those we never wish to go through again are lessons in themselves. Not only do they provide us with lessons that the soul can learn from, our worst experiences may be part of our reason for being here. Our world is a vast classroom, a training ground in which we are offered many opportunities to learn.

Even the dark times we go through may be beneficial, for they provide contrast and show us how to recognise the good that can be found around us. When life seems ugly, then it can serve to help us appreciate where beauty truly lies. When things are at their worst, we can recognise that the friendship, companionship and compassion we receive from others are some of the most valuable gifts we get from life. To give unconditionally, purely out of love and concern with no desire for reward is the embodiment of God's love and can be one of the hardest lessons for us to learn. We are part of our soul and our soul is part of us and, whilst we cannot always absorb and progress with all the lessons presented to us in the curriculum of each life, how we react to each situation is our pathway.

Did we but know it, we live in two worlds. Here on Earth, our greatest fulfilment comes if we are able to bring a spiritual feeling into our physical being. For our soul to progress in spirit world, it must know the full spectrum of experiences in a physical body. Only through an experience and understanding of human life can our soul progress and evolve. Without this input from our physical being, a soul would exist as a consciousness without the vehicle for progressing its development.

If we choose to view life from a spiritual perspective, we aid our soul's journey here on Earth. For without this wider viewpoint, this additional dimension to our thinking, we can fall into the trap of focusing solely on the material and the immediate. Then, if our present experience or our past history is emotionally painful, we may become cynical and expect from the world only more of what we have received so far. Even if we have had a relatively happy life, when we encounter problems, we can make the mistake of getting lost in our feelings and become confused, angry, negative or perhaps even bitter.

If starved of love here on Earth, the soul can be stifled and even suffocated by feelings of loneliness. Therefore, the experience of living without love can act as a signpost, showing us the value of interaction with our fellow human beings and the worth of relationships.

A spiritual viewpoint gives us options as to how we react to our physical and emotional challenges because it is the most unhindered perspective we can choose to take. It also means that, unfettered by doubt and less prone to negativity, our soul has a greater opportunity to express itself through our thoughts and emotions. True fulfilment is found through the act of being true to ourselves, not by allowing our negativities to hinder us. Therefore, finding out who we are can be a road to fulfilment, because we find out how to live with ourselves in the moment.

In the world of spirit, in our soul energy-forms, we can learn many things, finding out about different areas of life and existence, acquiring knowledge as we do so. However we can only encompass with our existence, and be aware of that which we have experienced in life. The experience of emotions, of physical pain, of loneliness or human love will be part of our soul's knowledge only if we have experienced it in physical form. So if life seems to be full of emotional strife, turmoil or longing, our soul is learning what it feels like to cope with emotional strains and negativities as a result and, ideally, how to put love and forgiveness in their place.

If we have not loved, we do not know what it feels like. If we have not experienced emotions or physical pain we cannot fully understand them in the world of spirit. Therefore our life here on Earth is full of experiences that can be of immense value, especially if we choose to treat them as such. Our emotions tell us how we are reacting, not who we are, rather we learn who we are from how we choose to react to our next challenge.

On Earth we have the chance to progress and develop in any number of ways and achieve material or spiritual goals. In spirit world we are progressing spiritually, so that eventually we might become a Divine Being with an understanding of everything that life offers us, both from the physical and spiritual worlds. If we choose spiritual progression as a goal here on Earth, this allows us to move nearer towards being a person we wish to be or to develop traits we respect, to be of benefit to life and to develop our capacity for inner contentment and happiness.

Sadly, in our search for spirituality we may find mountains that are hard to climb, full of lessons that can be tough the first time we recognise and accept them. Life is not easy for many people and when we recognise our role in it, it gives us clarity while we may feel things more keenly. Therefore, developing insight can mean we are more open to feeling the pain and hardship of life while we become more aware of its true potential. That is partly why the higher we progress in our spiritual development, the fewer beings we will find who we can relate to, because it can be a hard road and not everyone chooses to be on it. However, when we encounter like-minded spiritual people with whom we have a common understanding, it can feel more comfortable than our day-to-day relationships. While there is plenty of room at the top of the pyramid of spiritual development, most of us have a long way to go to reach the pinnacle.

It is wonderful to be alive and no matter what we feel is going on with us, imagine what it would be like if we did not possess this life.

Imagine what we would be missing out on if we did not have the potentials offered by a physical existence.

If we live our lives on a spiritual level, recognising the magnificence of everything in this physical existence, ourselves included, then despite the pains and miseries we might sometimes endure, we may find a renewed sense of wonder and even awe. Without a recognition that merely the experience of life can be fulfilling in itself, then by comparison our lives might seem two-dimensional. Unfortunately, we can interpret a lack of flavour, a lack of good feeling and a lack of depth in life as the true story. In fact, if we feel this way, what is really happening is that we are recognising the lack of an integral part of life, the giving and receiving of friendship, bonding and love. If we put all our insecurities aside and have faith in ourselves, we are better able to see the bigger picture. Then we leave ourselves free to recognise the role that even everyday experiences play. Then, even the little things can aid us in recognising the abundance of learning and good feeling to be had in the great scheme of life.

Understanding just how lucky we are to be alive is a cornerstone of living spiritually, because we can then recognise both the value and the significance of our life on Earth. We can only use our five senses because we are alive. Without life, we would not directly experience a tree moving in the wind, the sound of the sea as it laps the shore, feel the wind on our face, see the moon lighting up the night sky, nor sense the awakening energy of a sunrise as it alights on our face. Like experiencing rain after a long drought, physical life is the vehicle that allows us to directly relate to all these things, because we are part of that reality once more. If we consider what it is like to feel the absence of all these things we might take for granted, we can better appreciate our own luck at being alive and how we have the opportunity to share that joy with others.

Viewed from spirit world by a soul that has yet to have a physical life, they might apprehend all these things, yet they may not be able to comprehend or relate to them. So a soul needs to be born into a body to appreciate the immediacy and exhilaration life can bring, to experience the essence of what, from the world of spirit, we can merely see as if through a pane of glass.

Only by being here can we find out that fire is beautiful, yet burns, that we need to breathe air, that gravity draws us to the Earth and that when we fall, we feel pain. Yet, while alive, a spiritual perspective is more than just understanding that we are part of a wider physical creation or that our life is precious. Spirituality can teach us there is a reason for every life here on Earth, a journey we are all undertaking and help us understand that although our pathways may differ and diverge, everyone is seeking the same kind of comfort and happiness, as are we. The more we can relate to life and to other people, the more we can take joy in the good fortune of others, the less we feel we need to compete, the less selfish we need be and the less we have to focus on our own wants, needs and desires as the be all and end all of life.

If we open our minds to an existence beyond the physical and beyond our five senses, then we have opened a doorway to appreciating not only our own life, but ultimately, the wonder of existence for every man, woman and child on the planet and in the world of spirit.

At any point in our life, we may look for wider meaning, wonder what it is all about and seek the reasons behind what we are going through. This search for meaning is very helpful to our soul, because it is desperate to expand our conscious thought pattern into the universe and beyond; seeking answers helps it find a beneficial pathway and to then identify the reasons for our existence. The vehicle to our soul's progression is human experience and, therefore, the life we lead here and how we lead it, is of extreme importance to the soul and to the world of spirit.

The length of time we spend in spirit world between each physical life varies in duration. Yet the bonds we form with other souls here on Earth endure forever and survive into our spiritual existence. Even those ties that began way back at the time at which we were first born into the Earth plane last forever in the world of spirit. This means that each and every life is an opportunity to develop and to expand and create positive relationships that last into eternity.

As the child of God, the soul is, in physical life, linked with the physical body, which is itself a child of mankind. Like leaping into a well, we plunge into physical existence and its experiences, giving birth to an opportunity to feel life and experience emotions, both negative and positive. From one perspective, life is like swimming in a thick nourishing soup that can sometimes threaten to drown us, while from another it can seem like struggling in a raging river that carries us along with it.

The soul is born out of love from God into a form of pure energy, without physical existence and yet is constructed of cells in much the same way as we are in physical life. These cells are made, as is the soul, purely from energy. Yet, despite the soul's existence as a separate form made of energy, if we lived only as a soul with no physical body, we would have no opportunity to learn from life's experiences. The soul absorbs, like blotting paper, everything our human form experiences and learns from all of our physical lives.

Consequently we need physical life, without it we would be far more limited beings, in that we would have no opportunity to change and evolve. Physical life opens more than one doorway, it offers a soul the chance to attain a higher level of conscious thought by recognising the consequence of actions and it also offers a valuable opportunity to interact with other souls.

Like a cell within a body, the soul is part of a universal whole and with physical life comes an opportunity for purpose and a choice as to what that purpose might be. So, as cells within the body group together with a common purpose, so the soul, acting with a physical body, will experience life alongside souls on similar journeys. Like attracts like.

In our physical existence we can give the gift of fellowship and love and we can experience this sharing alongside the effects of its absence. So, through physical life, we can find encouragement and examples from those we bond with, as well as seeing the results of negative behaviour. Through friendship, we can encourage and help each other through life, aiding one another spiritually and physically. If your soul is seeking a particular direction and you are responding and living your life in this pursuit, then you will always find yourself in the best time and place to further your goals, yet these goals can only be fully realised once the lessons of this particular lifetime are learned.

So our soul wishes to be known to us, because if we can truly understand it and where it is from, we can become one with our soul in our physical life. Like a curtain being lifted, once we begin to truly appreciate that there is a reason behind everything, we can get so much more from the life that has been created for us.

When we pass over, we bring back what we have experienced and it is the emotional meaning of life, the spiritual feeling that is of importance, not the mundane everyday things, unless it is they that lead us to the experiences we are seeking. For there can be meaning found through seemingly inconsequential acts, such as making a cup of tea for family or friends if we do it out of love.

To the extent to which we are conscious, our soul has increasing choice as to which pathway it wishes to pursue in each physical life it is born into. It may have needs it wishes to satisfy and, in much the same way as in our lives on Earth, we may wish to pursue our development through creativity or the cultivation of friendships, so our soul may apply itself to pursue its interests. So, while the soul's overall journey is to learn so that it progresses upwards, on the other side we have choices as to what particular type of life may best serve to further our spiritual progression.

When a new soul is born into its spiritual existence in God's realm, it is an entity made of energy and has neither knowledge nor boundaries. The life our soul experiences there is a pure consciousness with no physical input. Yet in spirit world, every soul experiences a connection with the wider collective thought of all other souls and of God. There is a background knowledge within each soul that they are connected. In the same way that we can breathe without having to think of it, so the soul doesn't have to be preoccupied with this knowledge, it is merely there within it.

Our soul has a life on the other side, with the opportunity to learn and apply itself to study. Yet, like the difference between intellectual knowledge and hands-on experience, there is a distinct difference between the knowledge the soul acquires through its spiritual existence and what it learns through the experience of a physical life. To encompass its full potential, to embody and understand its own nature and the possibilities of existence, the soul must live it and, ultimately, while our soul may find knowledge in the world of spirit, it is only through human existence that it may gain the experience it seeks. The soul has to exist as energy because this energy is immortal. If the soul had instead been a physical organ in our body, it would die when our physical existence ended. So it has to enjoy a separate life form to preserve all the knowledge with which we enrich it. Therefore the ultimate purpose of our human life is to provide input into our soul so that it may grow and progress.

So each time a new baby is born into the world, it is bringing with it a soul that is eager to learn life's lessons. United together, the physical side of life teaches the soul, while the soul lends our bodily existence a spiritual element, gives us our purpose for being here and, if listened to, can provide us with perspective. It is for that reason that what we do, what we give, comes back to us twofold.

For, while we are alive, what we put into life provides us with returns on both a spiritual and a physical level.

When the spiritual is central to everything we do, we are consciously living life's ultimate purpose and following our soul's pathway of progression. For, if our physical actions have a spiritual purpose, then we are uniting the physical and the spiritual in a way that offers us ultimate fulfilment.

We call this ultimate fulfilment because, when we have lived spiritually, overcoming our self-delusions, our conscience clears, we work through our karma and bring love to the world, fulfilling ourselves on every level. This is the nearest we can come to 'Heaven on Earth', the state of grace we can achieve when we exercise our freedom of choice in a spiritual direction. Our twofold return is to be loved by spirit world and loved by those who recognise us here.

Chapter Two - Learning Our Lessons

For our soul to progress to the ultimate state of existence, it must navigate its way through all of human experience, so that we know the intense joy of love, the pain of loss and understand our emotions and for what reason they are born. Yet this progress, just as in life, is never smooth and we all encounter obstructions. All of life is connected and whatever we do affects all of life, ourselves, others and the planet on which we live.

Life is one experience, an expanse of existence that we can all enjoy and, while our reasons for being here are limitless, there is no one set pathway. Yet, there is always a primary reason for our coming to Earth, one overarching lesson we are here to experience. Perhaps we are here for family bonding, to set examples and show the way, to learn from others and their experiences or to grow and expand ourselves to the next level. We might be here to leave a heritage of our work, to experience what it is like to give, to enjoy life, to be a mother, father, leader, helper, giver, absorb knowledge, give birth or to gain strength through experience. We can come here to love unconditionally, to make amends, save another's life, care for the world, nurture animals or to express through art and music what lies within us. Whatever our reason for being here, life is the great teacher that will show us how best we might achieve our purpose and fulfil our goals.

Choosing a positive outlook

Each of us has a unique disposition we are born with in each life. Yet the effects of life and our choices will mean that we sometimes become negative. That, in itself, may be one of our lessons; bad experiences are there for us to learn from and can teach us not only lessons in themselves, but also help us learn that life can feel very uncomfortable if we get locked into our negative emotional reactions. While some experiences may seem hard, perhaps harder than we are able to bear, the most beneficial approach we can take is to look to each challenge and understand what it teaches us spiritually. If our emotions are telling us life is uncomfortable, we should learn to listen to our inner-voice, the soul and as we become accustomed to that enlightened viewpoint, look for what changes we need make. Often, our hardest lesson occurs when we learn to face our fears, or to avoid repeating the same old mistakes. When we reach that point when we have no recourse but to look to ourselves and the way we are reacting, we can seek an alternative thought process that helps us to enjoy what we can of life. Whatever holds us back, when we learn to move on and extricate ourselves from stagnation or an uncomfortable position, as a consequence, our soul progresses on its pathway.

None of us are perfect and as much as we might dearly love to live our whole life spiritually, our limitations restrict us. Some parts of life may seem hard and perhaps even too difficult to cope with. If our challenges are part of our chosen journey of learning, then in these circumstances we may come across the same problems time and again until we are able to overcome them, or our reaction to them. It is only when we have done this, that our lesson is learned and the cycle can be broken. Until then, it may feel like life constantly confronts us with the same problems and individual patterns of behaviour may repeat, manifesting themselves as discomfort, or as emotions that we would sooner do without. In each case, we should ask ourselves what an experience is teaching us.

The role of older souls
It is not only individuals that may experience repeating patterns, the collective behaviour of families and cultures can perpetuate in positive or negative ways. For instance, if a family line is continually engaging in negative behaviour, perhaps breeding violence, negativity, or abuse this can create an environment that is detrimental to the souls born into that family. If this ongoing story is to be changed, so that souls born into that line are not to perpetuate bad behaviour forever, then something positive must be brought to

the situation. An old soul may be introduced; one that has learned the necessary lessons and will not be influenced to adopt the relevant negative behaviour. This is because an older, or we can say wiser, soul will naturally move away from harmful or ignorant patterns that it has already experienced in previous lives. It will have a natural sense, an inherent understanding of what is conducive to a positive journey. Therefore an old soul may be born into a family to help that family break the mould, for the members of that family to see the possibility of another direction. The old soul could lead by example, illustrating that we need not merely be shaped by life, but instead can shape it. Yet such an old soul may experience a terrible time. Born into a world of negativity, a person with an old soul would sense the wrongness of what is going on around them and reject it while they are still maturing in their human form. Yet, their full influence may have to wait until the physical body has matured into its adolescent or adult physical form, when they will be able to act to change or set a new example. Once that person is old enough, they can act, directing their pathway in accordance with their soul's imperative. The worse the situation we are born into, the stronger we may need be to choose a positive direction. Yet, each time we listen to our innermost intuition, those feelings that are uncluttered by our doubts and fears, we allow our soul to share its voice and have the opportunity to guide us in a positive direction. The more we listen, the stronger that innermost part of us becomes.

Therefore, older souls, because of their maturity, can be chosen to fulfil more challenging roles. Because they are wiser, more tolerant and patient they may be put down here on earth to help immature, rebellious or lost souls in their own development. The more mature souls are therefore, guides to those younger souls that care to listen, while they too continue to learn from every experience.

Yet young souls do not necessarily pay heed. So for those older souls that are ignored, while this is not a failure, life may be a journey that does not achieve its primary purpose. This is one reason why we say an old soul can have a rough time on Earth, because while an old soul may possess inner-knowledge beyond that of those around it, their maturity may set them apart and be a source of frustration to them.

The purpose of our life's journey

The fact that we can find life's journey frustrating and seemingly hard work can give us all the more reason to find a way to learn to connect with our soul. For by connecting with our inner nature, we are far more likely to find a satisfying and rewarding pathway.

Without a spiritual perspective, we have only a limited vision as to our role in life and how we fit in. Yet there are many levels of self-knowledge, the body and soul are not separate, they are one. If we understand both the purpose this integration fulfils and our own ultimate potential for development and act upon it, whether we are making cups of tea for those we love, or climbing mountains, we can truly say we are living life to its utmost. In other words it is not the nature of what we do, it is the recognition of our purpose and acting upon it that is most important. If we are acting spiritually and pursuing the pathway that is best for us, it will be of benefit to others as a natural result.

We all start each human life with love from God and spirit world behind us. Then, if we are fortunate we will receive love from the family we are born to. If we complete our journey here with flying colours, we can return home at the time of physical death having fostered and nurtured that same love we started out with. Yet, we can be diverted, overpowering the guidance our soul provides and lose direction as a result. So our balance may go too far towards our own interests, our own goals becoming so important that we would do unto others that which we would not have done unto ourselves. If this is the case, we may feel strong, but our strength is being turned and used in a way that is ultimately damaging to us. This is because negative behaviour is in opposition to our life's purpose. If that life's purpose is delayed or rejected by our own will, then we will need to learn not only the lessons we came here to experience, but also make amends for that behaviour which is contrary to our journey. However we justify negative behaviour, it harms us inside and the world around us and most of us know within ourselves what is right and what is wrong. The good feelings we receive from helping others and from a clear conscience far outweigh the self-satisfaction we receive when we have sacrificed our principals or other people's well-being to meet our own needs. We need not think too deeply, pursuing a spiritual pathway is merely about being true to ourselves and doing unto others that which we would have others do unto us.

By contrast, those who are steadfast and sure, yet go with the flow, who, when life calls upon them to accept and endure, do not put upon the world, may lose out in physical life. If you are neither willing to subjugate, lie, deliberately manipulate another's feelings, nor steal to further your own cause, you run the risk of being downtrodden by those who will do these things to meet their own needs. The meek do not inherit the physical Earth, rather they inherit the rewards of a clear conscience. These rewards are immediate in that we have a better experience of ourselves and also more lasting, in that we are creating a Garden of Eden for ourselves in spirit world.

Considering the consequences of our actions, is not meekness, rather it takes far greater strength than riding roughshod over others. Those who recognise their own conscience and act in consideration for the effects of what they do, create a fertile ground, an environment that nurtures understanding and forgiveness.

By being true to ourselves and doing unto others as we would have others do unto us, we are naturally following life's purpose and allowing our spiritual side to develop and grow. We will also be creating a clear pathway for the spiritual to work through us. If life is challenging, instead of lashing out or fighting those around us, we can choose to express ourselves without creating malice or harm and we do not become part of the 'problem', nor create our own obstructions to development.

If we take this approach, everything that happens around us can help develop our understanding of life, how to deal with it and to better recognise the purpose it serves. Therefore, if we embrace peace over violence, we are a creator of peace. If we listen to those we see as weak, instead of shutting them out because of their limitations, we can learn from the suffering of others and develop a greater ability to get along. Likewise, if we are able to understand our emotions rather than be ruled by them, we are in a position to help ourselves and help others who are, in turn, experiencing trouble, turmoil or pain. By reaching out we can learn to attempt what may seem like an impossible mission, for if we make the effort, life can find ways of resolving even seemingly hopeless situations.

One secret to living a fulfilling life is to recognise that everything we encounter in it is part of the learning process. The more we are able to consciously recognise that life is furthering our development, the more we come closer to engaging the process of life as a whole, with its spiritual and physical aspects combined.

To connect truly with others, we need to develop empathy, an ability to relate to them, their situation and to put ourselves in their shoes. If we have gone through similar experiences then this can help. Only by having experienced all aspects of life as part of our reality can our soul relate to others and to life completely and this mission may take many lives to fulfil. Therefore, we need a physical existence, not only to advise the spiritual, but also to teach us how to relate to others, to understand their pain and in so doing, be able to move on. For once we have learned every lesson in each and every life and completed our curriculum, true wisdom and knowledge are gained. Those who accept life's lessons and learn personally from them, eventually transcend this Earthly existence and their souls are then ready to move on. Their souls are then ready to choose a permanent life in spirit world or to come down once more in future lives to help others.

We should not, however, think of this life as having no point other than earning future rewards. The benefits of a spiritual existence are not gained from self-denial, but from being true to you. We have already inherited a world of opportunities and going with the flow rather than fighting life means we have a chance to be ourselves fully. Spirituality is a pathway to being fully awake.

Therefore, life is far more precious than just the mere possession of it and we have the potential to create and destroy on many levels. Physically, emotionally and spiritually we can take ourselves higher or find ourselves sinking lower. Whether we recognise it or not, our spiritual journey is ongoing and what we do affects not only the here and now, but our immortal soul.

Transcending belief

The course we choose to pursue and what we choose to believe has consequences. If we think spiritually and act spiritually, we will at the very least be seeking a pathway of positivity and be more open to recognising spiritual phenomena, both in this life and when we transcend to the next.

If we firmly believe there is no spiritual dimension to our lives and it is merely a physical realm we inhabit, then when we pass on, expecting the blankness of dissolution, when we emerge into the wider spiritual life of our soul, we will find ourselves surprised. If we have denied the connection and were surrounded by like minds during our physical life, the shock of passing will be compounded as our soul's existence is made apparent and we find ourselves living in a form we denied during our Earthly existence. It will, therefore, be harder for our soul to communicate with other souls and those who think of us on Earth when we pass over than if we had actively encouraged the spiritual in our lives. Therefore, for a time, we may find ourselves estranged from other souls, until we have made the adjustment and acclimatised to a continuance of life without our physical body.

By contrast, if we have a background of being open to the spiritual, hold spiritual beliefs, or perhaps live in a community that practices spirituality, then we will be familiar with the idea that we will be emerging into a different reality when we die.

Having a community that is open to the thought of an afterlife can also help us in other ways when we pass. It is far easier for us to communicate with those souls who remain in the physical world if those same souls share our belief, for both sides will be prepared for communication and the transition won't come as quite a surprise, nor will finding our consciousness existing outside and independent of the body.

No matter what our religious beliefs and opinions, familiarity with the concepts can make the transition less surprising and the greater our understanding, the more readily we can recognise ourselves spiritually when we pass over.

However, it may be that we feel no reason to seek answers elsewhere. We may never have been challenged to the extent that we need consider a life other than the physical, or educated in a way that causes us to question. Whatever the reason, if we have no belief in God and no reason to talk to Him, no recognition of the spiritual side of ourselves, then we are living like a single cell in a body that has no conscious connection with those around it. Of course, we will have our physical interactions, our day-to-day down-to-earth business, but our lives are lacking a dimension that might otherwise serve to expand them.

Sometimes, therefore, hardship fulfils a necessary role, because it may only be when things break down that we consider alternative ways of looking at life, or seek help from sources we wouldn't normally consider. In this way, those who find themselves in trouble, beyond their means to cope, even if they have no belief in the spiritual, will often turn to God for help and therefore hardship becomes the catalyst for a search for greater meaning.

If we find our relationship with God and accept Him, then the wider connection we share with those around us becomes more apparent and we have the basis for our spiritual journey.

By living physical lives with a spiritual perspective, by taking lessons from the painful and embracing opportunities to give, share and love, we can learn to accept and move on that much quicker. Whatever level of growth and understanding we achieve within ourselves here, we have those positive attributes in our life on the other side. Eventually, after many lives on Earth, we may ascend to a permanent spiritual form. There, in spirit world, we have an opportunity to provide assistance, sending love and good feelings to those who are going through painful experiences. Whether it is for our eventual lives in spirit world or for our lives here, we need to experience life to fully relate to those who are experiencing pain. If we are to empathise with humanity, we need to understand all of human experience.

Whatever the manner of our passing over, when we do die, it is usual for us to meet with all those souls we have a recognition of, and with whom we shared life. So we migrate into our groups, recognising family and friends and souls that we connected with in life. When we pass over we will pass into the spiritual level we have attained, earned, and are capable of existing within. If we progress to a higher level of understanding, with a greater capacity of love than those around us, we have a greater choice as to whether we associate still within that level or whether we wish to move on to what we are capable of. The more self-awareness we attain here, the greater our self-awareness in spirit world and the more flexibility we have to move within levels. Moreover, at the time of our passing, the more we have recognised the spiritual element of our lives and have incorporated it into our thinking, the quicker we will adjust to that new life. With enough learning and progression, ultimately we can dwell permanently in spirit world, but in the meantime, we progress ever higher, recognising our journey for what it is.

While we have Karmic journeys, redressing past actions is only a part of their function; they are also a reflection of the fact that we must learn before we can move on, therefore karma is more about what we are doing now, rather than which we have already done. The more open we are to recognising that what we do unto ourselves and others has an impact, so we are more open to living a spiritual existence, one that promotes good karma and the more positive possibilities open up to us in that existence.

The more mature our soul, the more knowledge it will possess, so while many old souls have to endure tough lessons, they always bring with them the benefit of what they have learned in previous lives. This means that whenever we are born we come schooled with knowledge that will aid us. When we come into this life from spirit world, we will naturally not only bring with us the understanding our soul has gained from these previous lives, but our character, phobias, knowledge and predilections can all be part of what we bring. We are all here to succeed in surmounting challenges those we encountered in previous lives and did not overcome and those that we are yet to face. It is natural that who we are is a reflection of what we are here to achieve.

Understanding

If we forgive, it does not follow that we should forget. Forgiveness is the expression of our understanding and it is remembering that allows us to understand and embrace forgiveness. Therefore, we can understand and forgive past hurts if we choose, but it is the offence we forget, not the lesson we learn. By learning about our own weaknesses, we can understand those of others and, by understanding, we can recognise both motivations and limitations. Recognising the causes of other people's limitations we are more able to see our own and vice versa and this awareness is a stepping-stone in our progression. By being aware of the causes of behaviours that limit our progression, we can see how it is possible to move beyond those same causes. So, if we are continually faced with challenges that test our patience or understanding, once we have truly learned to be patient or forgiving and embody that positive trait, we have moved beyond that lesson. Therefore, life is ultimately very simple, but living it without recognition of its purpose can seem complex and challenging, when really the answer to life is to be flexible and to learn and live with love, because this brings not only the best feelings for us within, but also the greatest opportunity for progression on our journey.

The message of spirituality is to love one another, because that is the realisation of life's mission. To do so, we need to understand ourselves and our fellow human beings and it is this journey towards understanding, coupled with our need for physical survival and security, which creates the myriad choices we face. Love that has no reason, applies no conditions and exists for its own sake, has no limits and yet is very rare to find.

The woes we experience here do not trouble us in the world of spirit. There, our souls are free to experience existence without the need for the hardships of emotional and physical turmoil that are part of physical existence. In either case, love is our ultimate goal, our journey and that which aids our progression.

From the time our soul is born we receive input that aids our progression. If we connect with our spiritual essence and allow our soul to guide us, we can learn from every experience and enjoy life in the most beneficial way open to us. If we live in this way, we become a vehicle for love.

No matter what culture we live in, life was not always the way it is now. In the past, people lived differently. Many of us view the past as a time of barbarism, a time before culture and thought had matured to the elevated position they occupy today. Previous societies may have survived in times when life was more basic and when torture and capital punishment were still common, as was the acceptance of mass enslavement. We may feel that the world has moved on since those days. Yet the world we live in is far from perfect, conversely we may feel that past cultures lived in halcyon days of stability and spiritual awareness compared to the pressured societies that occupy the Earth today.

Whatever our view and wherever we feel we are in relation to the past, today's lifestyles can be demanding. Whether individually, or as communities and countries, too much pressure of the wrong sort; that with which we cannot cope, can lead us to seek solutions that, while they may mean our immediate physical needs are met, are in fact detrimental both to our long term future and to our spiritual development. Therefore a starving neighbour steals and is punished for trying to satisfy their hunger, while a scared child turns frustration at a seemingly hostile world into anger and lashes out with physical violence. Neighbours who could be friends, make enemies of those physically nearest to them, while we seek distance from our relatives and acquaintances because relationships are turning sour. However uncomfortable we may be with the way the world is apparently turning, the one thing we can be assured of is that we are exactly where we are meant to be. Even though we may find ourselves dealing with uncomfortable situations and the feelings that arise as a result, this generation and age, for us in the developed world, is about bringing our emotional states to the fore and to do so, we need situations that will challenge us. Yet, wherever we are born, whatever the nature of the life we live, there will be opportunities for us to develop ourselves by helping others. So, for instance, being born to a starving family offers opportunities for others to give to us and so one person's need serves as a chance for others to give. Many of us live in a developed world and our immediate battles of survival against nature are mainly overcome. This means our struggle for existence has changed, but still life's challenges remain and are exacerbated by the pressures of a growing populace, meaning cramped living conditions, frustration, starvation, persecution, war and the ensuing exodus of populations.

Although the realities of life are sometimes harsh, the tougher the challenges we face, the more benefit we receive from connecting with ourselves and who we truly are. A tough life means that being true to oneself is that much more relevant, because if we are not, we might easily become lost to the resultant negative emotions that hardship can bring. Knowing one's capabilities, limitations and the goals we are aiming for means that whatever situation we face, it offers a further opportunity to discover ourselves in our entirety. When the chips are down, if you know yourself, then you are more able to face the realities of any situation. A spiritual outlook enables us to face defeat, so that no matter what we win or lose, emotionally, materially, or physically, be it related to our life, our love or our livelihood, we can still have confidence in life and in ourselves and faith in our ability to accept and move on. Winning, in a spiritual context, is trying one's best, because that is the route to vanquishing all our inner hindrances.

Here on Earth, we are always, to some extent, actors on a stage, playing out the roles we have chosen that are appropriate to our journey, or even those parts that are thrust upon us so that we might fulfil our destiny. Even though we are acting out a life that serves a greater purpose, by being accountable to our beliefs and who we are, we will feel more in tune with that purpose and more secure as a result. True faith, that is based on knowledge that there is a bigger picture, introduces certainty into our lives. This certainty of knowing there is a higher purpose served by all of life can lessen the worries we feel in our day-to-day existence. This leaves us free to learn positively from that which confronts us and, by being true to ourselves and our beliefs, we become steadfast. This, in turn, means that we are less likely to feel bad because life has been hard, because our inner strength remains come what may.

We are spiritual beings taking a journey in a physical body. To evolve, our soul needs the body and our body needs the soul. By recognising this union, and acting upon it, we take an important step on our pathway of spiritual progression.

Learning through life's experiences

Our soul needs experience to develop and that experience comes through each and every life it lives here on Earth. Returning home when the physical body dies, the knowledge our soul receives from each human lifetime enables it to expand according to its actions and what it has learned from that physical existence.

Therefore, the ultimate reason for our being here is to progress our soul's journey and we do this best by living in a way that fulfils our spiritual needs. Life is a precious gift and if we embrace it we are fulfilling God's wish that we live it to the full.

Chapter Three - In the Beginning

Before there was God, there was an infinite blankness, a void without substance form beginning or end. Imagine an absence of all we know and take for granted. Within this empty space, no moon, nor stars, nor energy nor consciousness existed. Like the pause between breaths and an absence of everything.

This emptiness was unable to expand; its initial inhalation could not be taken for there was nothing to take in. In reaction, it then drew inward, folding in upon itself, until it reached a stage where it could draw in no longer. It condensed beyond what it was capable of sustaining, imposing itself upon itself, creating a pressure that could not be maintained nor released. This caused a giant discordance and inevitably, seeking outlet, a maelstrom of chaotic energy grew. Turning upon itself, into a circular vortex, space became a swirling circle, like a giant donut shape. This shape then revolved on its horizontal axis, and effectively fell through its own centre, the outside becoming the inside and vice versa. With the impossibility of so much energy occupying so small a space, unsustainable tension was created and a blast like a nuclear explosion on a cosmic scale ensued; a mushroom shaped energy formed and the beginnings of reality as we know it resolved itself into form.

So it was that, as the void fell inwards, exceeded its own tolerances, turned in on itself and imploded, all that was nothing became something. The resultant blast created a cataclysmic turbulence, an upheaval of everything that then spread in a moment, a tidal wave of matter distributing itself across all of reality in the blink of an eye.

After this cataclysmic event, the potential for God now existed but, as yet had no form, nor divisions within it. Like a single cell, it first divided itself, then multiplied again and again, growing and growing. Each of these cells was the potential for an existence, components that would naturally grow into the form of God as we know Him. So

God grew from all the potentials of this explosive event and was born into awareness from all these individual cell-like elements, each of which held the potential, like DNA, for Him. On a far greater scale than our own, God was born to awareness, so that he recognised Himself and, from this point forwards, all that we know today of the universe was assured of coming to being.

So, before there was anything, there was God and it was from the void that He came. He existed as an individual energy, alone in the universe, a Thought and a Force that encompassed all existence. There was nothing outside of Him nor beside Him.
With a metaphysical Big Bang, the consciousness of God came into being. Therefore, the first potential in the massive universe that was to come was its Creator. Before this time, before God existed, there was merely the potential for His existence. He was the substance of everything and the substance of everything gave rise to Him. Without Him there was nothing.

The creation of the physical universe was God's doing. He originated from this blueprint of created matter and at the same time, He is the blueprint, coming into being before time began, for He has no need of it. From nothing came God and from Him, the beginnings of every potential that we experience today.

From the point of fertilisation, when our own big bang occurs, cells divide and multiply according to the blueprint of our DNA. In the womb, our body grows and the physical vehicle for our conscious awareness first develops. So it is that the birth of each of our human lives mirrors God's beginnings.

Why we came into being
There are no accidents in the universe and all that is, is a natural consequence of everything that came before. So, all that is yet to come is also the natural consequence of everything that came before it.

We are all following God's journey of developing perfection and if we are consciously pursuing our spiritual journey, we are seeking to cast out and reject all that is negative, inviting only that which is positively good, recognising the faults to which we might be prone and dismissing them. Yet no matter how far we choose to deviate, cast in His image, we progress along a pathway set by our Creator. He invites us to love and nurture so that we might realise ourselves and take our natural place, a full and permanent existence in Heaven.

For, initially, God grew alone. Existing without any form of reality around Him other than Himself, He wished to progress, to expand, to interact with a consciousness other than his own. He created and nurtured children in His own image, so that He might experience the joy and knowledge that only come with parenthood and bonding. To provide a place for His offspring to dwell, He created a spiritual reality that we call Heaven.

With all of Creation as His domain, God could experience everything within it, but wished to expand through experience. Therefore, He needed to interact with reality in other ways and to do so, He created our souls, entities of energy born from God to populate His Creation. Then God created the angels; first amongst the spiritual life forms, the angels are beings who only have a spiritual existence in Heaven and the uppermost of the myriad levels that exist within the spiritual universe. These acts of Creation allowed God to deepen His experience through witnessing our development.

The first five souls

Originally, before our souls were created, God made five perfect beings that were initially limited to a spiritual existence in His world of energy. They knew God directly and yet, as they grew in understanding, they craved experience and wished to grow. This growth could only come by encountering that which challenged them. These souls were in a vast playground and they needed to interact with a life over which they had no direct control, for in God's world, that which they wanted was theirs.

They had no idea how He would bring these new experiences into being, but by asking for more, their boundaries needed to expand, just as He knew they would need a physical existence through which they might mature.

To create this experience, God created a physical reality and a physical world in which these beings could occupy physical life forms and experience actions and their results. The physical reality He created is our physical universe and within it, the Earth, a home for our souls and humanity to thrive and grow.

The Earth provided somewhere for these souls to explore their being, testing themselves in an environment where thought can create action and action comes with consequences, somewhere to love one another and to hold that which is dear and somewhere to experience themselves and learn.

By experiencing our physical journey, He could encompass more than just His own thoughts, rather could He feel, through our progression, the raw nature of our emotions and some of the nobility and compassion that makes humankind unique. In this way, He would be able to both grow and feel what it was like to create within his Divinity while nurturing the human race. Like taking on the responsibility of being a parent and all the learning that entails, God took on the responsibility of the entire human race. Through experiencing our successes and failures, He would create the causes for not only our growth, but His own also.

So, having created a physical reality, an Earth populated by life with Heaven above it populated by the angels, God had produced all of Creation as we know it and our souls took birth upon the Earth, fulfilling our craving for purpose and life. Therefore, as Creator, it is His power, His will and His thought process that guides the natural order of everything that is. As parent to us all, it is God who knows us better than we know ourselves. While we live here, our soul is the ultimate expression of our essence and its home is in spirit world with God.

When was man first born to the Earth?
Our souls first joined with physical bodies here on Earth hundreds of thousands of years ago. This was only possible once our early ancestors had evolved to the point where they were capable of conscious thought, when their brains were able to reason and integrate their impulses and emotions with the imperatives of a human soul.

The human brain is unique in that it is capable of original thought and of developing through its interaction with life to a degree far beyond that of anything found in the animal kingdom. It provides us with the ability to develop ideas, create language that will express these thoughts and to experiment through our interaction with the physical world and one another. It enables us to understand, to act upon what we perceive, to innovate and to explore.

The soul is that which provides the deepest stimulus for our complex thought processes and enables our personal evolution and that of the human race. It is the human soul's presence and its interaction with the brain which makes us human in every sense of the word.

The soul is aching for experience and the human brain provides it with the necessary tools to act upon its urge to awaken to understanding. However, in our pre-human ancestors, before they were joined with the soul, even for those that possessed a complex brain, there was no spark to stimulate the imperative to learn and explore. For without the soul, they were limited to basic impulses and the most rudimentary ways of approaching their environment.

When the first soul came into a human body, the brain and the human race was young. So the emphasis would have been on the spiritual side, for there was far less cultural or intellectual patterning to interfere with the communication between the first soul and its brain. Like donning a space suit, the first soul would have experienced an unimpeded connection with the body and physical reality. So, in those very first early days, we were in one sense far more spiritual in nature and it was only with the development of our cultural and intellectual structures, that the physical side of our lives began to hold sway in the human being. Gradually, over time, we became more human beings and less spiritual beings. At the same time, in the early days of man, much of what we did was governed by instinct and life would, of necessity, have been far more basic and even barbaric. Yet now, because of our intellectual progression, we are able to choose, to deliberately steer ourselves so that we can recognise our spiritual natures and enable the soul to have more effect in our lives.

From a spiritual perspective, a human being is that physical form which enables our spiritual journey. Just as it was necessary for the world to evolve to a point where it was capable of sustaining plants and animals so that it could support human life, so the human form needed to evolve to a point where its brain could sustain an intellect capable of meeting the needs of the soul. So man inherited the Earth, for it was the sole purpose of Earth to provide a habitation for the growth of our soul through a physical body. Therefore the primary purpose of our planet is to facilitate a spiritual journey, making its survival integral to our own. We need the planet not merely for our physical survival and for that of our children, but for the journey of all our souls throughout the ages.

When we first came to Earth, our human bodies and minds were very basic. Our souls first began to come to Earth into the forms of humans once we had developed a conscious thought process and had moved away from the purely instinctual drives that had governed existence before that. So once we had learned to walk on two feet and at the point we began to reason, our souls joined to bring love, beauty, balance and harmony to our existence.

At the outset, there were just the five souls, whom God created and existed with Him in spirit world and it was these five souls that wished for a physical existence that were the very first souls to come here and walk the Earth. One by one, once the world had evolved, they were born. Their first footsteps on the planet were, for them, like entering a virtual reality, a whole new world, accessed through their new senses. In spirit world they were perfect beings with perfect thoughts and yet here, like early explorers, these newly incarnated souls would test every emotion, every action, as the world of reality opened to them. Sensual pleasure through eating, interaction with one another, the simple pleasure of sensing the world through sight, sound, touch, taste and smell was a new experience that, of itself, offered the most incredible stimulus to these voyagers into the unknown.

The first two souls were born as a male and a female, while their three fellow souls waited until the time was right and then one by one they came. Each soul was born into the blood line pioneered by those first two souls. Each time a soul took this momentous journey, it entered into an amazing new reality, one which brought with it all manner of myriad new experiences.

So it was that we progressed. Initially two of the five souls came here with their spiritual essence intact, testing all the waters available to them. Over time they reproduced and new souls were born from God to the progeny of man, each one taking its place in the newly formed groups that would eventually evolve into communities and the beginnings of today's societies. The five original souls gradually came down to take human form, physical existence took precedence over the spiritual and every form of emotion was felt. So from God's five original souls, beings of energy born into a human form, came man as we know him today.

With physical existence came temptations. We wanted to experience, we found things attractive and lust, ennui, greed, were all born from our love of life. We fought, we loved, we killed, we gave life, we struggled for survival and wished for more. At the same time we lost the perfect existence we experience in our purely spiritual form. In coming into physical being, we also lost the awareness of our spiritual existence, lost the knowledge of where we originate from as a consequence of our coming here. This holds true today, where none of us are aware of our spiritual origins and only a rare few of us have an inherent awareness of our past physical lives on Earth.

Naturally, by living on the Earth, we have multiplied from the five original souls and as each new physical body came into being, so more souls were created by God to experience and interact. As a natural consequence and a stipulation for this kind of existence, every being possesses free-will, so that every action has unlimited consequences, in order that we may learn from our Earthly journeys.

Each act of conception can create a need for a new soul and as we multiply, more and more souls are brought into existence. Each and every one of us is pursuing the course originally requested by the five original souls brought into existence by Him.

One way of saying this is that in the beginning there was the universe with nothing in it, then emerged God who made Heaven in the fashion that suited Him. Then there were spiritual forms created, who wanted to progress, then God created man and the beings progressed through their physical bodies which enabled experience. At this end of the process we have inherited the bodies we live in and this life on our world. We are the lucky ones that have benefitted from all of Gods work to live here and inherit the Earth.

As entities, we are each of us like two pyramids that meet at the pinnacle. The bottom pyramid is our physical body, the top one being our life in spirit world. The point where we are joined is where we are born and pass over, like two worlds which are mirror images one of the other and this blueprint allows the progression of mankind.

Therefore, within our reality, God has always existed for He is the Father and Creator of all that we are and, while our human minds do not always recognise His existence, we cannot exist in His absence.

Originally, before our souls sought a physical existence, Heaven was formless, a beautiful world of colours, tranquillity and peace that we could move through effortlessly. After our physical lives took form, we could return to Heaven after each one and bring back with us all the positive memories. So, Heaven is populated with our souls and within it are all the expressions of beauty we recognise from Earth, physical life manifested perfectly in spirit world. So what were previously merely feelings and nebulous balls of energy, became trees and shrubs and plants and rivers, beautiful buildings and endless landscapes we identify as paradise.

Chapter Four - Proving God Exists

Wherever we are in Creation, it is not up to us to prove the existence of God to another human being, nor force the knowledge upon them. If we have no belief, that is our prerogative, but neither is it right to rob someone else of that which we do not have for ourselves. We should not seek to take someone's most dearly held belief, or that idea which is precious to them merely because we do not share it, for that which we have not earned, nor own, is not ours to take. For sometimes faith is hard fought for, it may be all someone possesses of value, or indeed the greatest thing in their life. Faith can hold lives, families and cultures together. That is not to say we cannot take issue with someone's actions or question them, but seeking to take that which someone holds dear is a crime, as is imposing our beliefs upon those who do not hold them.

Over time, God has played a greater or lesser role in our existence here. Nowadays, in the brief time-span we inhabit in this era, God is available to us in many ways. He can be found through the one-to-one communication of prayer, through our allowing our minds to be open by believing there may be more, seeking to add to life through religion or spiritual practice and even merely accepting through faith. We can reinforce this communication by reading and practicing spiritual disciplines, or sometimes we may suddenly stumble across Him and He becomes apparent in our life.

Some of us may be ambivalent to the question of whether God exists, neither believing nor disbelieving. Some of us may reject the very idea of a force in our lives we cannot currently see or sense. Yet others amongst us rebel, their anger at the way life treats them spilling over into blame that seeks an object. If we are lost, we can find ourselves casting about, trying to find a plan, a reason, or a power behind our existence.

When we are rejecting or blaming life, it is a sign we recognise our inability to control it and that it has dealt us blows we feel unfair. If this is our situation, it is a sure sign that we have not recognised there to be a bigger plan, order, or meaning within the universe. Alternatively, our circumstances may have called us to question the very nature of whatever faith we have. If we recognise that there could be a Creator, someone or something greater than ourselves, we may not understand how such a benevolent force could allow us to feel such pain. This attitude can be the first step to rejection of all spirituality or by stark contrast, a sign that we are ready to commence a search for meaning.

If you cannot find your own personal proof and therefore reject the very idea of God, it is still of benefit to keep an open mind.

God and the entire spiritual universe is made up of energy and we can either open or close the door to this energy by our attitudes. For God cannot impose Himself on us and if we are saying 'no' to God, then we cannot hope to recognise Him in our lives, for the very act of denial closes the door on the very energy that could let Him in.

A negative attitude towards God may block us from comprehending Him. Having a positive attitude can only leave us open to recognising His presence, yet still this will not guarantee that we will, for it may take time to do so. Our relationship with God, like any other is a journey of learning and communication is perhaps the most essential element within that bond.

Questioning God's existence is perhaps academic, for ultimately we can neither prove nor disprove it other than to ourselves. Yet, there is no requirement from the Creator that we recognise Him and we are not blamed for our opinions, but rather we progress based on our actions. It is how we treat each other that matters most and if discussion helps open us spiritually or refines and tests our opinions, then questioning God can have a very positive effect in our lives. Yet denying Him serves no positive purpose, for it limits the potential for us to find an ultimate fulfilment or purpose within our lives.

We should never seek to force our opinions on others, whether positive or negative and our true reward for recognising God or for helping others is who we are, not what we receive in recognition.

Yet, if we believe there is nothing outside of our physical existence, that is different to wilfully rejecting the idea of a God. The former limits our existence to the years between birth and death, while the latter may be a reaction born of a negative reaction to life. We may blame God out of a sense of hopelessness or anger because we feel our existence is lacking and we need somewhere to place the blame. Rejecting God out of anger is also a reflection of our frustration and a sign that we cannot imagine how life could change so that we can find peace of mind.

Having belief in something positive can add to our lives, but having belief in nothing leaves us empty in an area where there could be satisfaction and this is perhaps the saddest state to be in. If we reject the idea of God, we limit our existence and its possibilities to that which we already know, the extent of our imaginings and to what we can possibly conceive. If this is the case, anything that can be attributed to a universal Creator must be dismissed, perhaps along with anything else not already within our understanding. What stops us from imagining that there may be something greater? What stops us from allowing the possibility to intrude? For our own mental health we should seek to at least keep our minds open so we do not reject out of hand that which we do not understand.

The purpose of life is to learn and allow ourselves to develop. If we believe in God, we know that even eternal life is possible, for guidance comes when it is needed, when we are receptive, and when we ask for help, but only in a way that will fulfil our spiritual journey.

Whatever our view and whether we recognise the potential for a spiritual existence or not, spiritual growth can be achieved by being good to yourself and others. We need not be religious to be spiritual, nor need recognise God in order to help our neighbour, for all that we do to help those we meet will further our spiritual growth. To grow spiritually, all you need do is to extend every effort to be yourself, to love thy neighbour and do unto others as you would have others do unto you.

God's energy can manifest in our lives when it is needed, visiting us in a one to one encounter so that we are fulfilled, answering our prayers so that our emotions are healed and our eyes opened or providing our lives with purpose as we develop our relationship with Him.

From our side, we, as children of God, have more to do to help one another and promote peace on Earth. All we need do is wake up to the fact that we are a spiritual being in a physical body. If we call His name He will answer, for He has not abandoned us, instead it is we who can abandon Him for much of the time we are here.

The soul's journey

As with our physical life, the soul's journey has both a beginning and a purpose. Its ultimate aspiration is to embody compassion for the human race and all of Creation, a state of perfection that can take many lifetimes.

Our soul has its beginning when it is born from God into the spiritual universe. It appears as a new consciousness, a new energetic entity that emerges directly from God. This formless awareness is born into spirit world as the innermost essence of our being and is the template for all that we are to become.

Like a new-born baby, a new soul emerges fully formed in its youngest and most immature state. It has a huge potential to grow through the experience of many lifetimes, so that one day it may embody its humanity and become a perfect human being in a spiritual form.

Our soul will be born into many lives across many eras and all of time is open to it. We may be born into times of barbarism or renaissance, into areas where we experience nature or urban life and there may be journeys of beauty, hardship, survival and peace. With the human race multiplying and increasing, many souls are currently born into an overpopulated environment. If we visualise the Earth as a field, in previous times it may have been mainly nature that held sway, awash with greenery, but in this era it is absolutely filled to the brim by humanity and nature is suffering as a consequence. Physically we are crammed in, room to move is limited and many souls are beginning to feel constricted.

Those souls that are here to experience nature, those who crave solitude or merely to experience space without intrusion have less opportunity to do so. All this means that there are many people with a need for release from the confinement they feel. So, when our inner needs cannot be assisted through physical life, frustration can grow and leak into our everyday existence. So, we see many areas where physical overcrowding is creating societies full of frustration, into which many are born that do not feel they fit in with the culture around them. This means that there are many areas in the world where people have a lot of learning and adjusting to do before they are able to adapt to society. In the meantime, they are potentially at odds with their environment and as a consequence, they are vulnerable to making mistakes.

When God created us we were made perfect and everlasting, the spiritual form of our soul providing a continuous existence without end. A physical vehicle was needed so that we could grow and the interactions we demanded meant that we would join and procreate. As a consequence, we exist in abundance in physical form and because we have pursued this physical existence, too many of us crowd the planet and threaten to upset the balance of physical existence.

Alongside those who experience a lifetime of difficulty and trouble, there are those who do have the capabilities necessary to function in this world. Yet, seeing the pressures and troubles around them, they react by endeavouring to keep the world at arm's length, shutting out the woes of those suffering around them and instead, focusing on their lives alone. By ignoring the needs of society and attempting to shut them out rather than recognising them or getting involved, we have those who have the ability to provide assistance but instead live their lives for themselves alone.

As we find our life's journey, all of us will continue to learn through trial and error. As a consequence and of necessity, we may make many mistakes along the way as we seek our individual pathways.

Whoever we are, the demands of life may confront us with many decisions; often we may feel the need to take a shortcut, to avoid telling the truth or to take a liberty to get what we want. If we do not succumb to our weaknesses, then frustration or a lack of direction can always boil over into aggression, be it an inner war with ourselves or conflict with the world around us. Yet, whatever we do, be it telling a lie or using intimidation to force our view, we may argue that our motivation is a good one, or our need strong enough to justify the means. Regardless of our self-justifications, whatever we do creates our karma and, at some time, we will need to live through the consequences of our actions, their effects on others, on our mentality, our conscience and our progress.

The soul does not come down here to be negative or to hurt people, so when we engage in violence without reason, we are acting against our progression, moving backwards instead of forwards and creating negative karma instead of clearing that of the past. If we bring conflict into the world, choosing it over other options, we will also one day need to experience that which we have created.

Choose violence and we will have to make amends one day. If we are to progress on a pathway of understanding, we will need to know what it feels like to be on the receiving end of what we put out and recoup the ground we have lost.

Pressure does not necessarily always boil over and outwards through violent or unnecessary behaviour. If we feel there is no meaning in life, we can instead lapse into boredom and apathy. We can then compensate by trying to escape life's harsh realities, seeking potentially destructive short term fixes, such as drugs and alcohol. These intoxicants can cloud our minds and if we indulge to the extent that they take over, then they become a driving force in our lives, whether it be momentarily or in the long-term. If this happens, our physical existence can cease to serve a purpose for our soul's journey and the only lesson we are involved in is providing others with an example of what kind of life to avoid.

Whether we take a spiritual perspective or not, all of us can appreciate that pressure building within us needs to be released, while recognising that if we seek this release in negative ways, it will have harsh consequences. Yet life's purpose is not always found and many will spend their time seeking satisfaction, sometimes in any way that is available to them. So, while we can understand why violence, drug abuse and alcoholism exist, we must know that there are alternative approaches to life that will provide good feelings instead of bad, create positivity in place of negativity and allow us to progress rather than regress.

If we really want to find meaning and help ourselves, then we should help others in any way that we can. Even the smallest positive gesture we make can have a major impact on our day, while improving the lives of those around us. Over time, habitually helping others will conversely help us in many ways, in the way we feel about ourselves, those around us, and in the kind of world we help create. In this sense, giving creates all the causes for us to receive.

What is true on an individual scale is equally true for society and the world at large. The drive to take as much as we can for ourselves is having a negative effect. Nature has ways of cleansing itself and when the population is getting out of control, pressure builds and seeks an outlet, finding release in a way that can have a negative effect on a human race that is striving to populate the planet. The more of us that compete for resources and even the basics of life, the more conflicts and famine will ensue. For regrettably the pressure we are putting on the planet is too great and release valves will need to open.

So while on an individual level, the soul is here to work through its karma, experiencing the effects and necessities of its spiritual existence in a physical life, that physical life will vary in quality dependent on the conditions prevalent in society and on the planet at the time we are born. So, no matter how evolved our soul, it will still encounter challenges and hardship.

We have many physical lives and our soul's existence is never separate from any one of them, nor does it exist in a different universe, rather it resides on another level of reality, all the time linked to us. To serve our soul, this one life has a role to play and vice versa. Our body and our soul occupy the same reality, at different levels of vibration. While the soul is a separate entity, it is more a part of us than our own thoughts and ultimately, we are one. If we are progressing well, then our soul will be making friends with us, acting in harmonious partnership as we learn from each other.

Souls are born into the area where they are needed, creating a starting point and a destiny. There is a need for every soul to fulfil its position in the world. With its individual character and attributes, each one fulfils a requirement, for the world must have people of different dispositions for many reasons. So God gives birth to souls to populate all levels of Creation, each with a predisposition, a natural leaning. Those that are born into an area of creativity in spirit world will fulfil the need for free thinking creative minds. Those that are more down to Earth can fulfil the roles of engineers and builders, while the intellectuals, mathematicians, soldiers, nurses, artists and farmers are all born to the appropriate area at the appropriate time.

For life needs its teachers, its healers, those who provide food, those willing to fight, those willing to bury the dead, those willing to grow and those who wish to observe and question life.

The initial life of the soul, before it is first born to a life in a human body, is lived in spirit world. There it lives in energy, a life of pure consciousness, where there is no struggle to survive, merely a oneness with Creation where it can experience its own consciousness while it applies itself to pursuits and investigates areas of interest to it. These explorations are lived out in the ethereal energy of spirit world. There, the soul has choice, just as we do on Earth and it can seek higher or lower thought patterns. Just as on Earth, our soul's journey in spirit world can either elevate or demote it and dependent on the choices it makes, it will rise and fall. Yet in spirit world we do not change position drastically, rather the influence of positive or negative choices are small fluctuations, because in the world of energy we do not have the hard stuff of physical life to influence us, nor does the environment have the potentially harsh outcomes of physical existence. Instead, like swimming in the ocean, the soul has less resistance and can float in the world of the immaterial. By contrast, coming into physical reality is like walking on dry land. If we are born into a physical body, our thoughts are manifested into a physical universe, what we think can become action, having a more direct effect on our lives, our soul and our karma. So, once the soul has started its curriculum of learning through physical lives, it will then rise higher, or sink lower all the more quickly because of this link with physical reality.

What we do in life therefore has a profound effect on our soul. After each physical death our soul returns to spirit world and naturally gravitates to the level and area for which it is now most suited, for like draws to like. So, if in life, we live well and help those we meet, so our soul will bear fewer burdens and elevate when we pass over.

According to whether we focus on creativity, morality or sensitivity, so when we pass over, our soul will be drawn to the corresponding areas in spirit world. It may be that there our soul spends much of its time with souls with which it is acquainted, family and friends for instance, but it will also gravitate to those areas with which it has an affinity, allowing it to create and build upon its connections with other souls. So there are many different levels on which the soul can both start its journey and then subsequently occupy in spirit world dependent upon what we do in life and on what we focus.

Soul groups

So it is that when our soul is born from God into any one of a number of levels, so it will find itself with souls of like-character, groups of collective mutual thought. Perhaps it will be born into a supportive family of souls that seek fulfilment on a spiritual level or one where the goals of the soul have degraded and the material takes precedence for those souls within it.

For those souls who have evolved enough, such that their primary motivation is to have a positive influence, their group will be defined by the common goal they share. This could be, for instance, to have a positive effect on the planet. While in spirit world, this group would project their feelings and thoughts to us here on Earth. When members of this group are born down here, they will be people who relate readily to the natural world, rather than being predisposed to materialism or greed, people who naturally want to help the planet or who have an affinity with nature. Equally, there is a collective thought in spirit world, comprised of souls that wish to help people who are suffering. These souls can send thoughts of love, seek to influence the world to direct aid to countries, areas of famine or perhaps aiding countries with thoughts of peace. So, our soul's primary motivation will determine which group we gravitate towards, actively seek out and find ourselves in. The thoughts we have to help those around us, or the planet as a whole, will be expressed by our soul whether it is in a body or between lives in spirit world.

Just as a soul can be born to any level or area, so we know that a baby may be born to any social, financial or emotional type of existence. Of course, our soul will have its own leaning, a journey for this one life and perhaps a purpose to fulfil other than the mere experience of it. So, each life will provide input from experiencing just who we are and the challenges that confront us. For it is very rare to find a life that does not challenge us in some way, be it physically, spiritually or, as we increasingly find today, emotionally.

Therefore, whatever faces us, there will be a reason. We may be here, for instance, for a lesson to be learned, for a positive impact to be made, for a life to be experienced or a message to be delivered. Therefore, no matter what we face, we can find a positive, if we are born to a negative situation in our physical life, perhaps being brought forth into a world devoid of emotional warmth or where there is an absence of love, this may present a great opportunity for the soul to grow through the trials it experiences. If, on the other hand, we are born with an emptiness within, then we may seek to fill our lives with love and it is learning the difference between a life lived with love and without it, that is our journey.

Regardless of our particular life goal, all of humanity, each and every one of us, has a great drive to belong and bond and every one of us is searching to fulfil our life's purpose. At the same time, we are all seeking to fulfil those blueprints that come with us into life, such as finding a mate and furthering the human race.

Recognising that we are spiritual beings first, living in God's realm, can enable us to take a unique perspective on life. If we adopt this attitude, it equips us to find happiness within, no matter what outer challenges life throws our way. Then we can grow, learn and progress quite far spiritually in just one physical life.

A lowly starting point, or a journey of hardship may be the very catalyst which directs the soul to recognise the value of love and friendship. For sometimes these two are the only things we possess. Therefore, a journey of confrontation and struggle is likely to help the soul to recognise the value of a spiritual outlook, or at least of camaraderie and friendship, either because we are feeling its lack or we have embraced it and found its worth in our lives. The more we can find love within ourselves, the more we are able to give. If we cannot find happiness or love within, then how can we give it?

We may begin as a soul with no great advancement and yet no particular challenges or born at an elevated level where we originate as a soul already self-realised and more aware of its own strengths, weaknesses and limitations. Wherever we start, all of us will feel, at our innermost core, a need for progression. How we pursue this is up to us, yet for life to be truly fulfilling, we need not shape the outside world to meet our requirements, but instead should seek to live honestly and in true harmony with ourselves, our needs and those of others.

It is difficult for us to fully comprehend the bigger picture of our lives, our purpose, the nature and structure of our soul and why we are here on Earth. Yet there is a source of wisdom behind everything and we have the ability, through our soul, to connect with it.

Our soul has the ability to connect with God and the spiritual universe to help us find and pursue the right pathway for us so that we might progress spiritually. It possesses the knowledge gained from past lifetimes and its own thought process, which we experience as our innermost feelings.

Therefore, the soul manifests as a voice or overwhelming feeling within us, to which we can all learn to listen. It is an energetic entity, a part of us that has a structure and a way of expressing itself to realise its goals. For we are not merely our everyday thoughts worries and concerns, nor our pastimes and diversions, we are also that part of us which bears the wisdom of past lives lived.

Allowing our soul to be heard helps us in our lives. Yet to let go of our intellect and logic, to allow ourselves to be open to life and follow our inner feelings, can seem a scary prospect when most of us spend so much time structuring a life that is under our own control and an expression of our own will. So, when we talk of surrender in a spiritual context it can be frightening, the prospect of letting go of ourselves, our human will and our usual way of operating. Yet, it is this act of letting go that enables the higher Will of God to act through our lives, guiding us in a far better way than we alone are able, for God recognises what is right for us. Our struggles are small and insignificant when compared to the bigger picture.

When we become frustrated by life, by allowing God in to work with us, we are allowing change to take place and things to move on in the most beneficial way for us and for our soul. We experience our soul's thoughts and wishes as a guiding wind, manifesting as our innermost feelings and an instinct to realise them. Pursuing this imperative is our ultimate purpose and to most effectively do so, we need to attune ourselves to our true nature and act upon it. Yet, we can become confused by attempting to logically find and pursue this inner-voice; the surest route to realising our soul is by recognising our emotions. By practicing compassion and love, we fulfil our soul's ultimate purpose, but along the way we may have many challenges and diversions put before us.

We must also bear in mind that God's concern is our inner wellbeing, not what we own or earn. Therefore, it is our reaction to life, our spirituality and who and what we are, that He is concerned with. It is up to us to look after our physical and material needs while ensuring we follow this bigger plan. Surrendering our will allows God to work through us, so that our reactions and actions are guided and, as a result, we can feel better about life no matter what is going on around us.

The soul is the seat of everything that defines us and the more we connect with it, the quicker we will progress in our spiritual curriculum. It is our choice to make whether we are true to it and seek ultimate fulfilment, or not. We are fulfilling one part of our soul's purpose merely by being alive, for physical life provides the soul with a boarding school in which to learn.

Our brain provides us with the ability to form thought patterns, an intellect, and the ability to connect and interpret the physical universe, so that we might meet life's everyday necessities. Our whole physical structure is a blueprint that allows us to pursue these physical needs. However, being born with this capability means that we can pursue our desires to the extent that they divert us, and even become consumed by the pleasures that are to be had through their fulfilment.

Often, meeting our physical needs is mistaken as the main purpose for our existence and yet it is up to us what goals our life fulfils. For our motivation is not dictated and our intellect can listen to our soul and choose to follow its guidance, or we can pursue our everyday desires, even to the extent that we risk conflict with our souls purpose. The choice is ours.

Every soul has a current level of progression and a level it has attained in spirit world. In each physical life, we may live in a way that can elevate or demote us. Like a bird, our soul is born into each physical life from the nest of the womb and when the physical body dies, it migrates back home to spirit world. By making negative choices and living badly, we fall and effectively drop a level in the world of spirit. By pursuing lives that harm others, we demote ourselves and lose sight of those we previously bonded with in spirit world and the position where we once belonged. If this occurs, our soul will feel an urgent need to return to the Earth, redress its previous wrongs and elevate itself once more. Yet, there are no guarantees in physical existence and if we face battles or challenges to which we react badly and miss our goal in the next life, we may yet again drop down a step or two. If this occurs, when we return to spirit world we will be immensely disappointed and wish to elevate ourselves once more.

Our soul's journey is one of hope for ultimately our true destiny is to progress upwards and just as we may fall, if we listen to our inner-voice in each life's journey, we can continually rise. For there comes a point in each journey at which every soul will come to learn its lessons spiritually. From that point forwards, having experienced this connection, the soul will invariably pursue a pathway that is positive to it and whenever that soul returns to Earth, its lives will have a beneficial impact. Whether we have reached this point or not, once we are pursuing life in recognition of our soul, we have the opportunity to progress. Each time we embark on the flight of life, ultimately we only have our inner feelings to trust and these reside in our soul. Progression is learning to think of others and to care for them as well as we care for ourselves.

Whatever our circumstances and motivations, there is always an element of chance in life and it may challenge us so much that we choose a negative pathway. Our soul would never want us to make war or harm one another, yet many of us succumb to the frustrations of feeling overlooked, alienated or unloved and turn on ourselves or others. If we lash out emotionally then it is bad enough, but much of the physical violence instigated in the world is the result of a lack of love and understanding.

Progressing on a spiritual pathway can call upon us to face hard lessons. Yet help is on offer. There is more to life than the way we are experiencing it right now, more than just our emotions, our opinions, our intellect and the input of our five senses, all of which are so obvious to us. If we learn to develop the spiritual gifts we are born with, we can appreciate and become more conscious of our intuition and the help on offer from the world of spirit.

Spiritual experiences
Regardless of whether we choose to consciously develop ourselves spiritually or not, there are many relatively well known spiritual phenomena that many of us can relate to, regardless of our beliefs.

One such phenomena is a process commonly referred to as 'astral travel.' We call it astral travel because while our body sleeps, our soul leaves our body and joins with the spiritual world, so it is like travelling out amongst the stars. It is a good example to look at because normally we think of spiritual experiences as being strange or seemingly unexplainable occurrences that happen to us when we are awake.

With astral travel, it is us, our soul, that is creating the spiritual experience by leaving our body and visiting some area of the spirit world. We may regularly travel to spirit world in this way, or it may happen rarely or never and where our soul chooses to journey is driven by our situation and needs at that time.

Life is our journey of learning and sometimes our soul has need of spiritual input. It could be, for instance, that we are in a situation where our soul is at odds with what we are doing in life, it merely needs guidance, or to learn more about life as it is progressing. The soul might then travel in our sleep and return to spirit world's learning places, where highly realised souls are all available, dedicated to meeting our spiritual and emotional needs, offering education and recuperation for our soul. There are classrooms with teachers of a high spiritual level to help us develop or counsellors to help us deal with difficult situations. So our soul may spend time in a classroom with a teacher that has experience in the area we are addressing in life, or conversing with a wise spiritual counsellor that will help it to absorb a particular lesson. These visits can help to strengthen it, or simply provide more energy so that the soul can maintain its purpose. For, over on the other side, it will be amongst all the familiar energies that enhance it and allow our soul to rejuvenate, so that we can deal with life all the better.

Alternatively, the soul may take an astral journey as a vacation from the body, to allow it to once more be among souls that are known to it, those with which it has shared a bond, both in life and between lives. So, it may go and meet friends, family or loved ones who have already passed over.

Another reason for astral travel is so that we might rescue lost souls. With so many of us passing over every day, there are inevitably a comparatively few souls who become lost on the way back to their home in spirit world. So those who are relatively spiritually progressed may journey in their sleep to help guide these souls back to their pathway, so that they can fully leave the Earthly plane and return home.

We may make these journeys regularly, but we would not necessarily be aware that we have ever taken an astral journey. However, sometimes when we awaken from astral travel, it can be very obvious and feel like we have fallen from a great height into our body. We have the physical sensation of falling and then wake up with a jolt as our soul returns. Generally this is because the body has woken up before the soul has fully arrived and we feel a falling sensation.

Visitations from spirit world

Whether we recognise them or not, spiritual teachers, guides and healers may journey to meet us here in our waking life. We will not physically see them and it is this type of visitation that many of us may recognise as the second way in which the world of spirit can connect with us. When a teacher or a guide visits us in our waking life, we may have a strange sense that someone else is present or there is a dream like quality to reality. It is rare that we will actually see them, but we are all able to feel to some extent when they are present.

Achieving life's purpose

There may seem no rhyme or reason to life, yet it all serves a purpose. The soul does not always recognise when it has passed its tests or made its sought-after achievements down here. For instance, it may be that life seems tough, or lacking in purpose, but all the while what we perceive to be an uphill struggle may have taught us the value of perseverance or to appreciate the finer things in life, such as friendship and love. Spiritually, we may have learnt patience, not to bear grudges, to live without animosity, never to be bitter, nor pass that burden of resentment on to others. We may not recognise it, but by keeping positive in this way throughout life, we have earned a very valuable achievement. In our search for meaning and purpose, personal peace of mind can be one of the hardest attainments to achieve. It involves working with our self, positively questioning our perceptions of life and making an effort to release the negativities we can otherwise quite easily find ourselves holding onto. For by merely avoiding the natural reactions that can make us negative and not taking them on board, we have achieved a very worthy goal.

We may naturally find ourselves living a positive life in this way, taking on board beneficial ways of thinking without labelling our journey a spiritual quest. As a result, we may act very well during life without recognising our own forbearance or good heart and it may be that when our soul returns home it can find itself on a higher level than expected, like walking through a doorway and finding oneself on the peak of a mountain instead of the floor of a valley. Our soul may therefore may be elevated when it passes over, without understanding why it has achieved its progression. However, this feeling won't last for long; in the spiritual universe there are myriad levels and wherever we arrive at the time of death, we will soon recognise and bond with the life around us. No one is left alone or abandoned on the other side, no matter what area of the spiritual sphere we end up in, nor what level or quadrant we occupy. We have put ourselves there and will come to recognise what is around us and, if we connect fully with ourselves, will also understand why we are there. Wherever we are in spirit world, we have no one to thank but God and no one to blame but ourselves!

The way in which we experience time is different in our spiritual and Earthly existences. Life down here is very short compared to the eternity of our soul's continuance and it is partly for this reason that what to us, may seem like a lifetime could be experienced like the blink of an eye to the consciousness of those whose souls reside in spirit world.

On the other side, our soul prepares for each life, gravitating towards an opening which meets its needs, desiring to manifest and feel, all the while bound to accept the requirements of its karma. So our soul is seeking experience through life and it is necessary to experience the price of this seeking, the recompense for its good deeds and the reactions for its past actions.

In the same way that we come down here with an agenda, we may have passions in this physical life that we take with us into the world of spirit. It could be, for instance, that down here we wish to paint or to excel at some form of creative art but, if this dream is not realised, when we pass over, we will take that ambition into spirit world. There, nothing ever dies, rather the energy continues forever. So, if our physical life ends, we can take these inner aspirations with us and seek to master those pursuits we loved in life in our spiritual form. There we may complete our masterpieces, creating for ourselves in an environment where we are surrounded by the love of God. In this way, nothing is ever lost in life nor does any creative ambition go unfulfilled.

How we experience death
Death is the natural conclusion of a physical life, a time when our soul returns to a purely spiritual existence. The experience of death

can be felt in myriad ways, dependant on the manner of death and the state in which our soul leaves the body.

If death occurs when we are prepared for it, perhaps at a time of illness or old age, we may feel ready to move on and the soul can leave naturally. If we are prepared, as the soul separates from the physical, we will be met by loved ones, greeted by those familiar to us who have passed over before and guided by them to our allotted place in spirit world.

Naturally, when we die there may be a fear of letting go of the body and, if this is the case, we may experience death as a tunnel. At the end of the tunnel will be everyone we recognise from life, those we loved or cared for, waiting at the end of the darkness and encouraging us toward the light in which they stand. They will show themselves in their Earthly forms, recognised from the time we spent together in life and we will feel all their love, drawing us towards them. The tunnel is our own fear making letting go seem all the harder.

Another way in which we experience passing over occurs when life is suddenly and unexpectedly taken from us, perhaps by accident. If our passing occurs in this way, then because of its abrupt nature, we may experience shock and find it difficult to accept and assimilate the fact that our mortal life has ended. Of necessity, our soul will need assistance and time to reconcile itself to the transition that has occurred. In this case, we will be met by souls strong enough to embrace us and whose role it is to take us somewhere we might heal before we are acclimatised to our soul's new existence and surroundings. In this way, even if we are in a quandary or disorientated when we pass, we will be guided to a place where we may recuperate.

Another way for us to pass over is when, at the moment of death, we perceive a glorious white light ahead of us. We are drawn in and taken up towards it, feeling the most central part of us, our soul, more real even than our body, as it is pulled into the brightness. This is an incredible and pure feeling, the most amazing feeling we can ever imagine. From the moment we perceive the light, we will forget our bodily concerns and be compelled to travel to its embrace. The light has a quality to it that makes it more substantial than any Earthly light, with a reality that we are not used to feeling in our everyday life, perceived without limitation. Drawn to this light, we should remember that we are being taken to our real home and that when we go there we may do so with our faults abandoned and our joy realised.

Were we to look back at the time of death, from our new spiritual perspective, we would see our physical body as being of no importance, as if it were a coat we have discarded. Those who have faith will find this transition easier to accept than those who have rejected or failed to accept the reality of our spiritual existence. Therefore, how we experience death is partly a result of how we have lived our life and partly due to our outlook. Seeing a white light is natural and it is only our own fear that puts obstacles in the way, a reflection of the fact that we are relating more to our bodies than the spiritual energy that is beckoning us.

Another way of passing is for us to be welcomed by the angels. When the angels come for us it is sometimes a reflection of the fact that we are spiritual, but they also come for children and the young. So, the angels will always be there for a good soul and the innocent and yet it is the need that is the predominant factor. Therefore, someone who has emotional and physical pain and lived a reasonably good life may also be received by the angels. To be met by the angels, we must also be open to their nurturing presence. However, if there is a loved one on the other side who can fulfil the needs of an individual's soul, then there may be less need for the angels to intervene to guide them home.

All of these distinct ways of our perceiving our passing are merely general descriptions. There are any number of ways we may feel the moment of transition and an infinite number of variations within these scenarios. What is important is we understand where we are going and trust that it is a natural part of our journey.

The experience we have as we pass over is a result of the life we lived down here, what we believe and how physical death takes us. The manner of our soul's passing is not the same as the manner of our physical passing. Our perception of our death is a reflection of who we are inside, how we have chosen to act and how much good we have brought to the world through our patience and love.

Chapter Five - Called to Account

When we pass, every one of us will be called to account for our deeds, so that we can address them and, where necessary, make amends.

It is our immortal soul that experiences this assessment of all our actions and, where appropriate, we are judged for both the good and the bad. Every part of our existence is exposed at this moment of reckoning and we will feel the full weight of any acts of deliberate harm we have committed, alongside the natural realisation of every moment we spent spontaneously helping others.

Those who have lived a life of conscience, having respect for life and putting their best into it, freely giving of their effort and good will, they will pass this review with flying colours. For them it will feel as though someone has opened a window in their minds, so that the sunlight comes shining in. This opening feels glorious and at that moment when we share our inner selves without guilt, we encounter a feeling of immense expansive bliss that fills every fibre of our consciousness. Our praise for a life well lived, when we pass over, will flood us with good feelings, which is a reward for everything we have put into life.

By contrast, some of us, before we even have to worry about dying, look forward with fear, nervous of being judged for past actions and regretting the harm we have caused. Therefore the thought of death is worrying and the idea that we might be called to account and meet our Maker, even more so. If we have done wrong and deliberately harmed others, then we are right to live in trepidation of having our deeds exposed.

Yet, if we are feeling this way, then we are already on the road to recognising our mistakes and, if we vow to not repeat them and seek earnestly to make amends, we will have hope of finding peace within, both now and later when we pass over. Even when we feel the need to make amends, we are still accountable for every action we have committed and our wish to redress the balance would need to be made real, either in this life, when we pass over, or if our karma remains unbalanced, in a future life. Everything we do creates immense ripples, for ourselves, for those who are directly affected and for those who hear about what we have done. Therefore, we need to fully feel the effects of every action; if we have made sincere effort in this life to make our wrongs right, still we might be called upon to experience some small shade of what we have dealt out, but because of our contrition, nothing as extreme as that which we might otherwise have faced.

For the purpose of judgement is not punishment, it shows us where we have gone wrong, to help us recognise and learn through our mistakes. However, our redemption does not come without effort. We must deeply wish, with all our hearts to make amends, to not repeat similar acts, acting on our remorse and regrets to ensure we do not repeat the same errors. If we find ourselves in this situation, having made heartfelt attempts to make up for past errors and mended our ways as a consequence, when we pass over we would be recognised as a child that had learned through harsh experience and emerged as a more mature soul. For realisation of ourselves is the goal and our time of judgement is a stepping-stone on the journey of our soul.

Whether we lived well or lived a lifetime of wrongdoing if, during our time on Earth, we have seriously wronged another human being, we will face scrutiny by spiritual beings who will weigh our actions in the balance. The purpose of this scrutiny is to show us those actions that have harmed others and to judge those that were carried out with malicious intent. For us to be whole we must experience all of our existence and be accountable to it. Therefore those who have wronged others must redress and those who are innocent and have been wronged will need to experience that which they were denied.

For the most serious acts and the grossest transgressions, there is a panel of supreme spiritual beings, three men and two women, all immensely powerful spiritual souls who sit in judgement of those lives where significant wrongs have been committed.

Being lead before them, in a single moment of knowing, the whole of our existence is experienced as we are laid bare. So our whole life flashes before us, that we may see what we have realised and that which we have not. Everything we remember and everything we may have forgotten, but they already know, is shown. This testimonial serves to awaken us to our good deeds and wrongdoings, as well as the effect we have had on those around us. If we have harboured ill feeling and acted upon it, none of our justifications can retrieve the effects of what we have done. Nothing is hidden from this review and all of us are open to examination, should our lives warrant it. Crimes we have wilfully committed against our fellow man will be assessed and whatever misdeeds we have committed will need to be put right.

All of our behaviour creates situations and if it has been detrimental, even inadvertently so, it carries on beyond our death. The stones we throw into the water cause ripples in the pond. What we do is passed on and affects others, especially those things that we teach and that which we instil in our children, which may have an effect for generations to come. It is only in subsequent lives that we can right the wrongs that remain unaddressed and truly make amends. If we do not have the opportunity to directly redress the balance in a future life by helping those we harmed, then we will need to live a life that will redress the imbalance we have caused, perhaps feeling the effects of similar acts upon ourselves. So, either we make amends, or we feel the effects of our actions, sometimes an element of both, so that we may fully realise the impact of what we do. Once our wrong actions from one life have been righted, perhaps several generations later, so our soul may free itself to move on.

If we have harmed others, if we have stolen or domineered, in whatever way we have done wrong, we will need to experience the consequences of it. From the most extreme behaviour of maliciously destroying another human being to petty lies and greediness, all are thrown into the balance alongside all of the good we have brought to the world and we are judged upon our actions alongside our intentions, each one according to its weight.

In extreme cases, where we have chosen to live a life of malice, one where others have constantly suffered as a direct result of our deliberate actions and we have brought no good to the world, we will have affected our thinking and emotions drastically and we may face very serious consequences.

So life is like a college and those who expand and grow will have a profound positive effect on their consciousness, while those who turn to the ultimate extremes of negativity will reduce themselves.

As we sow, so shall we reap on every level of our existence.

If we have lived a harmful life, entirely devoid of consideration or respect for others, dealing out hurt and injustice with total disregard for other human beings, then our soul will have nothing positive to experience when arriving home to spirit world and will be called to account.

The panel of judges we can be called upon to face when we pass over is not in that sense like a judge and jury in the physical world and not everyone faces them, they are there for the more serious misdemeanours, where a decision has to be made. There, in this court, everything is self-evident. While here on Earth the truth must be extracted and fought for, in spirit world it is merely revealed to us. On Earth we may justify our actions and while we may, to an extent, be ruled by our emotions, when we pass over we see the truth of our behaviour revealed without it being clouded by our justifications or rationalisations.

We cannot bask in the glow of solid achievements if we have not had any and we cannot live in contentment if we have done wrong and not made amends, rather it is natural that upon confronting what we have done, we must exist for a time in regret.

Once our actions have been recognised, for every type of negative action we wilfully commit, there will be a price to pay and each one reaps its own form of disgrace and reckoning.

If we have lived a life of the most severe negativity as someone who has a lack of regard for their fellow humans, then what we receive when we pass over will reflect this way of being and we will find a debt to repay. It may be we will need to experience emotional estrangement in a future life and upon passing over, we will need to feel what it is we have caused in others and to experience it for ourselves. So we may be cast into a void in spirit world, devoid of loving feelings and experiencing desolation and anxiety until we are ready to return.

The human body is just a vehicle and the soul can come back many times. However, there are many 'big crimes'; things that will generate the most negativity. The biggest crime of all is to break someone's spirit, to deprive them of their free speech and freedom of action, or to rob them of their will to live.

When a person who has gone to this extreme and maliciously crushed another's will passes over, they will need to experience what it feels like to be treated in this way. This is the way the universe works, for without consequences, we would not know to choose the right pathway and without karma, we would not be accountable. We need to understand in our soul what it feels like to receive love and also the pang of emotional pain, so that we learn to fully embrace and accept love unconditionally.

So if we have gone to an extreme in this way and taken another's free will, when we pass over, we may be put into a dark hole, where existence is like walking blindly in an echo chamber. Here, at this level of existence, whatever the soul encounters, it does so without awareness of what it is. Like bumping around blindly in a pitch black room, whatever the soul bumps into triggers a reminder of something bad they have done. This is a reflection of our being blind to the needs of others, of having stripped them of their ability to express themselves and making them fearful of every encounter with us. So, by deliberately stripping someone of the very essence of their life and their free will, we will experience in spirit world, the horror of an existence where we are consumed with fear at each encounter.

If we have committed very bad acts and we then extend every effort, emotionally, mentally and physically to make amends then there is the hope of redemption. If we have corrected things down here, then when we pass over we are redeemed so that we might start again. For God never gives up and everyone aligned with Him in Heaven will do their best to help us on the other side, to help us find the life that is right for us.

The soul grows and the more we live a life that reflects its needs, the faster that growth takes place. If we, in the denser physical plane of Earth, make choices that are guided by an aspiration for life to be better for ourselves and for those around us, the soul grows faster than if we are limited by our fears. If we are progressing in this way, in conscious recognition that we are far more than the sum of our physical parts and choosing to go with the flow whenever the option would be to react negatively, our soul grows.

If we achieve the highest level, when we pass over, we travel upwards, seeing our journey as a tunnel or staircase. There are many ways of perceiving this crossing point to the other side. Sometimes we are directly transported by guides or our loved ones who come to take us, but however we make that transition, we find ourselves directly in the level which is most appropriate for us. If we have achieved level seven, our passing will be the least shock of all, because to be here we will already be a spiritually minded person and much of our thought is conscious and open, while what waits to receive us on this level are the most divine of beings. That being said, even at that level we can pass suddenly and without warning and if that is the case, then we may need a period of readjustment before we are open to the spiritual reality we now solely exist in. So guides may come to us to take us to a place of healing as we arrive. On level seven we then find ourselves on God's ultimate level for the human soul to inhabit and from that point forwards we may continue our journey in spiritual form.

In spirit world, our soul might be born the size of a pea, but with a physical life well lived in conscience, we have the opportunity to grow to something the size of several football stadiums.

All God's Children

We cannot learn all of our lessons in one short lifetime, it is next to impossible to incorporate all of the experience we need for the development of our soul in a single lifespan. That is why many of us have already lived many lives and those many new souls who are coming down to Earth will have lifetimes ahead of them in which to learn. So life is a great gift that is far more wondrous than we can begin to imagine. All of us are butterflies waiting to be reborn into spirit world, where we bring back the beauty of a life on Earth as a gift to our soul. Each baby that is born to us is a gift from God with limitless potential, not just for what it achieves for itself materially, but what it is doing for its soul through the act of being, what it might bring to others and what we might learn through that baby's life. For while we may be parents, each of us has an ultimate child for which we are responsible, the soul which exists within us.

Children can be hungry to discover and explore life and this instinct that craves involvement, brings the soul the experience it also needs. Being part of a child's growing-up years is a great opportunity to witness how the physical body, our intellect and our emotions mature and take on their own individual identity. It is also a unique opportunity for us to begin to understand how the right influences can have such a major and lasting impact on any life and how, if we choose to share and care for our children as best we are able, helping them to grow, it enables the growth of our own soul, creating a little piece of Heaven on Earth, where love and patience are the guiding forces.

While each child can have a very specific reason for being born, for its own soul's development, it can also have a purpose it serves for its family. So an old soul in a new-born child might bring with it the wisdom a family most needs, while a young soul in a child might need the wisdom of old souls, found in parents that will help guide that souls' future. For, while a child has no control over its formative years, it brings with it the inheritance of its soul's experiences in previous lives and the spiritual awareness it has gained in spirit world.

We must always remember that we are all children born to God and that we are, all of us, made in His image. He gives birth to the spiritual and we give birth to the physical and born to life in this way, each and every one of us has a connection with His realm.

While this is the way we are made, the human condition is such that we have no conscious awareness of our soul. Just in the way that we have no conscious need to regulate our breathing, so the soul is merely a part of us. To understand ourselves and the role we play, we need to put in conscious effort and that effort is normally born of a need, an imperative to find some greater meaning and purpose in life.

When we begin an Earthly spiritual journey, the only reference point we have is what we find with our five senses, how our emotions react to our life experiences and how we rationalise our lives intellectually. All of us are affected by our culture, the media and the opinions of those around us. Even if we rebel, we may then be defined by our decision to reject that which would otherwise indoctrinate us. For those few who enjoy true freedom of thought, the very direction of those thoughts, the tone of our consciousness, whether we are positive or negative, all these things are products of our past history in present and previous lives.

We all hold opinions and these are fed through life's experiences; if we open our minds to spiritual thought, we add to this limited equation. We can come to quite startling discoveries, finding we are much more than we imagined, that we have limitations we did not expect and that we are loved come what may. We can find that our opinions are formed on bias and not fact and that the past is useful in that it informs our choices for the future, but that no matter what we experience, it doesn't determine who we are; only we can do that by choosing what we do next.

Spirituality can only be a personal journey, because each of us, our consciousness and the way we think, is unique. Yet, we need reference points and some form of structure to help us learn, otherwise it is easy to become lost, or imagine that because the universe is limitless, that anything goes.

To help us relate to God, many of us imagine Him in human form, as a man or a woman, a He or a She. For the highest level of consciousness we are aware of resides in the human form and to comprehend that there is a consciousness behind Creation, we will often visualise a human being. We think of Him as a wise old man or a Mother Earth figure because we relate to the human form and to people because that is what we understand.

Just as we may visualise God in a human form, so if we are fortunate enough to have an experience of Him, He may hold that form for us to help us relate to him and understand that He has a consciousness, a Will, a thought process and a voice. If we saw Him merely as a glowing ball of light, or an energy field, or perceived him as the emotional feelings he projects to us alone, then we might find it harder to relate to the feelings of Love and

Compassion He holds for us. For He shares our experience as fully as we know it.

We are cast in God's image and He is the blueprint for our physical form. Our bodies are a universe of cells that we encompass with our skin, just as He encompasses the universe of spiritual and physical reality within his consciousness. While God expresses Himself through the universe, we express ourselves and relate to His reality through the micro universe of our five senses and our bodies, which are our physical vehicle to reality.

As Children of God, we are born in His image.

How we behave

Thinking and acting spiritually enables our soul to expand. If instead, we are purposefully ignorant or act maliciously towards others, we will have to come down here time and time again, until we learn to give the soul a chance to introduce a spiritual feeling into our lives.

We should not feel that every bad thought or inclination we have is a cause for punishment. Merely experiencing a mental wish will not cause harm to another. Therefore we should not punish ourselves for thinking ill thoughts. However, if we spend our lives thinking negatively we will be punished here and now in that we have created a negative and limited mental environment that will serve no purpose other than self-harm.

However, if we act upon our thoughts, then we will have brought them to fruition and they will have an effect on someone other than ourselves. One of the interesting things about negative thoughts is that they can become obsessive or a source of very cold comfort to us. Positive thoughts, by contrast, uplift us and are not subject to being replayed obsessively in our heads. So, the two types of thought can be clearly distinguished in this way. They also reveal their true nature in that positive thoughts do not trap us in mental loops and therefore do not hold us back, while negative thoughts can enslave us in our own fears and insecurities so that we are never able to move forwards.

If we pursue a negative course deliberately and maliciously so that it harms others, at some level we will be conscious of it, for everyone knows when they are doing wrong, be it when they are deluded, through drink, drugs, rage, or self-justification. If we persistently pursue a negative course to an extreme extent, by taking delight in harming others or causing them pain with complete disregard for their feelings, we can ultimately diminish our soul to the extent that it dies within us and deprive ourselves of our chance of everlasting life. What we give out in life we get back twofold.

When we are born into this life, the underlying feelings that come with us will be, in the greater part, a consequence of the karma of previous lives. So it is that we all have an inner awareness of our karmic journey, a subtle feeling inside that provides the impetus for us to choose an appropriate direction, an impulse to pursue the most beneficial pathway. In the same way that a bird may feel the need to migrate, this inner guidance is an imperative in our soul that manifests as a feeling or an urge. If we feel an overwhelming need to help the planet or other people, this may be something we neglected in previous lives, or it may merely be that we never got the chance to realise that goal. If we come to this life seeking love, it could be that we never had the opportunity to express it in a previous life, or if it constantly eludes us, that we acted in a way that deliberately deprived others of the chance. The inner needs we have, to be loved, to develop friendships or helping others, are guides that can direct us towards positive actions, bringing help to others or love to ourselves and those we know. Yet we may feel the lack of fulfilling these needs as loneliness or frustration and therefore, it is always our choice how we choose to react to our emotions, whether we are imprisoned by them, or whether we act to the very best for ourselves and for everyone.

The human condition is such that when in spirit world we live in an environment where everything is achievable, we can relate to one another and love is readily available without the pain of human life. When we are born into a human body, we may seek this feeling we miss so much and the bonding that comes with the unconditional love our soul is seeking. The contrast of human life, where love is not guaranteed and we can lack this closeness, can make us all the more aware of its value. When our needs are not met and we encounter the vagaries of human beings, it can lead us into suspicion and mistrust. Yet, while it is natural for us to be cautious in the physical world, the feelings we seek can be found inside ourselves if we choose to progress along our chosen spiritual pathway. For like attracts like.

In this age on the planet, right now, our karma is coming back to us far more immediately than in past times. We are living in a time of spiritual awakening, where spirituality is readily available to many people in many forms.

If only we could live in love and bonding here, the woes of the world that we lament so much would pale by comparison. Looking at it in this way reveals not only the full extent of what is missing from many of our lives, but also how, if we choose to focus on a common higher goal, life can be so much better. If we are able to bring love to our families and friends, to put stock in relationships and to truly care, then life would be far better for all of us. Instead, there is a temptation to dismiss those around us, to reject, to focus on the negativities and to get lost in the feelings of yearning for that which we do not have. If we are brave and put value on our relationships and invest in them, we are passing on a valuable example to those who know us.

There is a basic curriculum we are here to learn before our soul may mature sufficiently and progress to the more advanced levels of inner knowledge. When we do advance in this way we become an older soul, more wise in ourselves and alive to the idiosyncrasies of human nature.

There are many ways of looking at the role of older and younger souls. All older souls were once young and those young souls that progress will all become older souls in their time. It is not necessarily how many lifetimes we dwell on the Earth that dictates our level of maturity and therefore wisdom, but it is what we have taken as a positive learning from our experiences. A soul may have many lifetimes on the Earth before it chooses to learn anything positive, or it may make so many negative choices that the soul is recycled at the time of its death.

Our soul must return numerous times until it has absorbed the fruits of all the interactions available to it. In the same way that in physical life we readily learn to read, write and process arithmetic, our soul's basic lessons are always available to us. As we go higher, the lessons we need to learn may become more refined. If our soul has learned love and honesty, it may still need to come down and learn how to remain true to itself, how we can juggle with many demands on our time, how to deal with disappointment, or a lack of recognition. It may need to learn to possess great power by being a leader, coping with the inherent demands, while remaining true to itself. For the soul that wishes to progress, the opportunities to experience the necessary lessons are fewer than those less specialised. To learn deep compassion, the price of fame, or how to handle power over many people, it will need specific situations that, in the same way as if we were seeking a place in a specialist college, are all the harder to come by.

Our soul then has to wait for the right lifetime to come along and such places in the University of Life can still be hard to come by. Conversely if we arrive too soon, while this may be part of the plan, sometimes the world is not yet ready for the experience a soul is here to convey and we witness people who are seemingly far ahead of their time, bringing information or lessons that are a hint of what is yet to be brought to the planet.

When we procreate here, it is like turning the key in a car, igniting the chain reaction that begins life. The creation of an embryo creates the need for a soul which takes its place in the womb. This natural process is as quick as lightning and as natural as breathing.

All of us on the planet today were born and all of us are destined to die and we all appreciate that in a hundred years, comparatively few of us will remain alive. So what seems so permanent to us, is merely one more moment in an ongoing chain of events. So it is that the physical world is in tune with the energy of the spiritual universe and natural disasters occur when the planet is threatened and the population of the world is as a consequence reduced. As with all physical deaths, souls can be taken up before their time, but all souls will in time be re-joined with physical life in the embryos of babies yet to be born. The creation of life and the endurance of love is the overriding imperative of the universe.

Recognising that we occupy just one small moment of time in the history of the universe can help us to put our life into perspective, putting our everyday worries into their rightful place as we focus on the bigger picture. In the annuls of history there are billions of lives from time immemorial, spanning the entire history of the human race, from when our souls first took human birth. Connecting with their stories can help us put our own into perspective, just as it enables us to open up our spiritual senses. Connecting with the lives of those who have passed over can directly awaken us to the reality of the spirit world, that nothing in life is unknown and that our spiritual life is as much a reality as our physical one.

The Hall of Learning
Sit comfortably and take some time to relax and allow your body and mind to settle. Feel your breathing become steady and allow all your cares and concerns to fade away. In your mind's eye, visualise

your feet standing in a hallway on thick red carpet. Look up and you will see elevator doors ahead, set into a wall in front of you.

The elevator has brass doors that slide open, inside it too has carpet that is deep crimson in colour. Stepping inside, directly in front of you is an oblong brass panel with one button at the very top of it and one at the bottom. You press the very top button and the elevator begins to climb to the very top level. Watch the lights above the door as the elevator climbs up each of the levels in sequence. You reach the top level, the elevator comes to a halt and you watch as the doors slide smoothly open.

You have now reached the level of the Hall of Learning. To your right and left a corridor stretches away and ahead you see another corridor with a small booth in it. Stepping out, you find yourself on yet more luxurious red carpet.

Looking further to your left you can see the corridor leads to the largest set of double doors you have ever witnessed. Despite the corridor being of a normal size, these doors are enormous and like an optical illusion they stretch upwards into the dim distance and at either side extend far to your left and to your right. Like Alice in Wonderland, despite the doors being near to you and seemingly of normal proportions, the closer you come to them, the larger you perceive them to be and stood before them at arm's-length, neither can you see their edges, so distant are they and so immense their size.

On these doors are carvings representing the history of the entire world, mankind's journey from its very beginnings to the current day. Images, landscapes and every major event represented in their entirety, carved out in deep relief on the doors and with every age imprinted on them. Running your hand across the surface, you can feel each and every moment of time committed to the doors. Allow yourself to experience and explore for just a little while and get a feeling for the immensity of the history of the human race.

When you are ready, turn and return up the corridor. Leaving the doors behind you, you turn to your left and find yourself at a small booth, a tiny glass walled room that sits opposite the lift.

At a desk inside the booth sits a man, at once grey-haired, ancient, vibrant and full of energy. You approach the booth and ask respectfully if you might have a ticket for entry to the Hall of Learning.
Smiling, he passes you your ticket and turning around so that the lift is now in front of you, you turn to your left, walk down the corridor, keeping the double doors behind you. Then, almost directly ahead of you, you come upon a throne, standing on a dais above two steps. Standing before the steps, you see a light shining out of a corridor to your right. Stepping into that corridor, to your left you find the same ancient man once more sitting at a desk. Presenting your ticket for the Hall of Learning you ask permission to enter and to hear a story from spirit world, the life story of someone who lived down here on the Earth-plane.

Smiling, he leads you deeper into the side corridor and you follow him, making your way to the Hall of Learning. Almost immediately you emerge from the corridor and find yourself in a massive room, the ceiling stretching up far and away into the distance and to either side, rows and rows of bookshelves, each shelf full of identical leather-bound documents, each the size of a passport. Within each book is written the story of a life, a complete record of an individual's existence, from the moment they were born to the moment of their physical death on Earth.

Absorb the enormity of it all. Myriad tall, wooden library cases carry billions of identical books. Walking between them, still following this ancient library keeper, you are amongst the life stories of every person who has ever lived on the planet throughout eternity. As you walk, before you, you can see one book protruding from a shelf. Pausing, you take this one book out from its allotted space and placing it between your palms, concentrate on the story within. In your mind, begin to feel that person's full life story as it is revealed to you.

Trace that person's life story from birth to death and feel their personality, their traits, likes and dislikes as they are revealed to you. Then, when you are ready, ask for that person to come and stand before you. Feel them approach and see their presence in your mind's eye. Do they present themselves as young or old, are they male or female? Note what they are wearing and their physical attributes. Allow them to converse with you. Feel them communicate, as you gain impressions of what they did in life, what they regretted and what they achieved. You may gain a sense of whether they died at a young age or advanced years. Find their family relationships and friendships, how they felt and whether their life was fulfilling. What do they most want to convey about their life? Do you sense that they felt life was an adventure? Were they most concerned with having a strong family? Did they absorb themselves in their work? What did life mean to them? Take some time to explore the feelings that you receive and the impressions you gain.

Then, when you are ready, thank them for allowing you to share their story, bid your farewells and watch this person turn and walk away from you, fading into the distance.

Then, return the book to the ancient man who will, in turn, return it to its space. You follow him through the library to his chair, where he returns your ticket to you. As he does so, give your thanks and ask permission to revisit, he will answer in the affirmative and, with this consent to visit in the future, go back once more to the small booth opposite the lift. Give your ticket back to him and enter the lift to descend once more to the ground floor. Return and open your eyes in your own time.

Chapter Six - How We Experience Reality

To begin to appreciate that there is more to life than merely the physical, it is helpful to consider the limitations of our current perception and how that restricts how much of reality we recognise. Here, we live in a physical universe and our bodies are constructed in a way that enables us to interact with this three-dimensional world. We need the physical bodies God has created for us, for through them, we have inherited the Earth and without them we could not function within it. When we live in our spiritual forms alone, we perceive reality from a vastly different viewpoint, for our soul and its spiritual existence is far different to this physical reality. By inhabiting denser, more solid matter, we have in a sense limited ourselves, for to learn about existence, we must focus the glorious expanse of our soul into the cramped quarters of a human body.

By its very nature, physical reality is limited and opening up to a spiritual existence requires us to go beyond the limitations of our current perception. By the same token, we cannot negate there being a spiritual existence merely on the basis of our not being currently able to perceive it.

To fully appreciate that there is more to the world than meets the eye, that the universe may have other dimensions, or exist in a different way to that in which we currently perceive, it is helpful to explore the limitations of our own current understanding.

Because our physical senses are only able to connect with the physical, we may believe that things we cannot verify with our physical senses do not have a 'true' existence and that the three-dimensional physical universe is all that there is. That is to say, everything in our universe and the physical objects within it are clearly defined, with definite boundaries, a place where they are and a place where they are not. Therefore, we may naturally believe that everything exists in this way that an object is either 'there' or it is not. We prove this to ourselves by looking, touching, smelling, tasting and hearing. So, an object exists if we can sense it through one of the five senses or augment our physical perceptions to 'prove' it is there, such as by using a microscope or a telescope, or sonar. Therefore a car is a car, a table is a table and a faraway star is thought to be a gaseous mass because we have been able to observe it and examine how it compares to our known theories, deducing its nature through processes our scientists have proven by the same techniques, reliant upon the same sense perceptions. If we believe that these tests are proof, that things must have physical presence to exist and can be proven only by using our physical perceptions or only once they are proven to our intellectual minds, then we should be prepared to test whether we can fully understand the way in which our universe physically exists by the use of this yardstick. If we can perceive and understand the simplest facts of our own physical existence using measures, dependent upon our intellect and five senses, then we have proven that physical reality is all there is. We would then have every reason to be able to use our own limited perceptions to judge everything of a spiritual nature and quite rightly believe that the limit of our physical perceptions is the true limit of all there is.

In reality, we cannot even encompass our own physical existence with our minds, because the rules or perceptions we are using are too limited.

Here is one simple way of testing. Use your imagination to cast your mind outwards, travelling in a perfectly straight line, up into the sky, past the moon, out past the planets and then travelling further and further to the boundaries of our physical universe. Keep going, imagine moving past all that is known to us and go beyond. If we believe in a three dimensional universe, then naturally, at some point we must come to the boundary, the edge of our reality.

Then ask yourself what lies at the end of this boundary, what is beyond it? At the same time, how could there be an end to the universe? What could be beyond it and where would that end? If there is no end to reality, no boundary, then that means our physical universe goes on forever. From our three dimensional perspective, this is impossible because nothing can go on forever in the physical universe. Therefore, if physical reality has no beginning and no end, the way in which we perceive it must be limited, or fundamentally flawed. There must be another dimension to existence that lies beyond our understanding, one where it is logical for physical things to exist within a far wider framework that has no need of boundaries. It is illogical for physical existence to be all there is to life, because this view depends on there being an inside and outside to all the totality of existence, a boundary to contain it all; that which is contained, must be contained by something outside of it and therefore physical existence cannot possibly function or exist in the way we imagine it to – for what contains the container?

Therefore, there must be a wider, more encompassing perception that allows for the physical universe to exist within a wider universe. In the spiritual universe, it is possible for things to go on forever, because energy can permeate and exist independent of the physical layers of reality. The physical universe is a limited expression of something far wider and greater.

For our conscious minds have no limit and neither does God's spiritual domain. Whereas physical forms begin and eventually end, energy can continue without cessation. In the spiritual realms, spiritual growth happens as part of the natural process of development and our spiritual forms have a continuum of existence that allows them to grow, even when they are not in physical form.

The nature of time

A useful question to ponder is the nature of time here and on the other side. We need to understand that the linear nature of our existence plays a role in defining how we think. Here we identify beginnings and ends to things both physically, in that they occupy three dimensions, but also temporally, in that things start and ultimately finish. There, in spirit world, by stark contrast, is a world without end. There, this lack of cessation enables us to experience our consciousness without limitation. The soul holds our deepest awareness and its purpose is to evolve.

Within the dense reality of physical matter in which we reside, time passes comparatively quickly. On Earth and in spirit world we are, in effect, occupying different realities. Above, in spirit world we are beings of energy where time has neither boundaries nor relevance and our consciousness has the potential to live forever. On Earth, it is a different story; we are governed by a daily cycle of sleeping and waking and of pressures that stem from our physical needs. To eat, to converse, to cater for our needs, all these things take time and ultimately, our time is limited for we enter into the world sure in the knowledge that we will one day pass from it. Therefore, the two worlds have an entirely different feeling to them. One is a world of pressures and limitations, while the other is a boundless existence that expands to encompass all we are capable of being and where love radiates upon us from above.

When we embark on the journey of a physical life and come down to Earth from the spirit world, our fellow souls may just have noticed our absence in the time that we have lived out an entire life and are ready to return. Time down here serves a purpose, in that it allows things to exist in a physical way. Without time, there would be no beginnings and no endings; for here in physical reality, every form has the need for a time to start and a time to finish. Yet we can still appreciate that this is a very limited existence because, as we have found, things cannot ultimately have the beginning and end we imagine. Likewise, in our physical form, we may only recognise our existence as extending from the time we emerge into it at birth and when it finally ceases at the time of death.

However, this reality, dependent upon the five senses and our intellect, is not all there is, for before and after our physical time on Earth, our spiritual existence continues.

If we want to understand this better, we must first open ourselves to the possibility that there might be more to life than the physical. If we are able to allow this, then this state of open mindedness, paves the way for a spiritual outlook, because we are accepting there may be more to life than that which we perceive with our five senses and have learnt from our own experiences. To directly appreciate that this wider reality exists, we need to find ways in which to connect with it. By developing our clear vision, we make it possible to perceive this wider spiritual reality. We can then verify for ourselves that there is more to life than that which is accessible through touch, smell, sight sound and taste.

Enquiring into the very nature of existence is not the sole preserve of spiritual practitioners. Scientists and those who dedicate themselves to investigating the nature of reality and time may reach a stage where they too believe there is more to the universe than physical constraints and our current understanding allow for.

So, while a necessary part of our spiritual development is to question the nature of our existence, this enquiry is something that many people can relate to, whether they refer to it as a spiritual quest or not. Once we have allowed the possibility that there is more to life, we can question to a point where we recognise that our current perspective is extremely limited. Appreciating our own limitations in this way is the basis for us to embrace a very real and pragmatic humility. For if it takes effort to even phrase the questions that allow us to get a glimmer of the wider reality that exists, how limited must our minds be in this physical form. For we do not perceive and understand the beginning and end of time, rather we are involved in our own present moment, wrapped up in our thoughts or dealing with the necessities of life that are part of being human. We form opinions from this life that can sometimes serve to limit us or occupy ourselves with day-to-day concerns that are mundane or trivial in comparison to the immensity of the universe around us. Even if we have progressed and developed our psychic senses and use the resultant clear vision to access this wider reality, we are still looking through a mere pinhole. To fully embrace spirituality, we are called upon to stretch our perceptions to bring us into contact with a level or reality that is higher than our own. Yet, while mankind is limited, our human form fulfils a very real and necessary function, bonding in a union with our soul to provide the vehicle for our spiritual progression.

Letting go

As the unknown becomes more familiar to us, it begins to hold less threat. Developing a spiritual understanding of life and recognising the limitless nature of our existence can help us to lessen our fear of death. "Yea though I walk through the shadow of death, I shall fear no evil." This lessening of our fear is the outcome of recognising the endless nature of our soul and also that there is spiritual help available if we allow ourselves to be open to it.

Moses asked "let my people go" when they were under the thrall of the Egyptian Pharaoh and eventually they were released out of their servitude. Similarly, a spiritual outlook can help each of us to gain personal freedom, because we are seeking release from the imprisoning limitations of life, our misconceptions, fears and impulsive natures. Recognising the bigger picture of a universe that offers us an eternal existence means we can gain freedom from our attachment to the things that would otherwise hold us back and offers the additional freedom of a widened perspective, no matter what our circumstances. For each of us can become 'enslaved' by varying degrees to the thought processes we develop which are based on fear and our reactions to life. Imagining that physical life is all there is and that we are limited in some way or other all serves to put us at the mercy of a misguided view. Therefore, developing your ability to 'let go', while widening your understanding of your own existence and what is possible can be the most liberating part of your life. Of course, this is not necessarily an easy or instant process. In the same way that the Pharaoh changed his mind and set his armies upon the newly freed Israelites, so it is easy for each of us to fall prey to doubts and consider returning to our old thinking patterns. It is the sea of our own emotions that we must cross if we are to find true mental freedom. In order to part that sea we must be willing to leave behind that which keeps us imprisoned. This is not an invitation to abandon thought or rationality, rather it is an indication that what we currently hold to be the limit of possibility is merely a function of how we are thinking. The true mountains we climb in life are those we surmount in order to widen our own viewpoint; true freedom is available and each of us holds a personal key to the Kingdom of Heaven.

Creation

There is a wider story to the Creation of existence than that of our own reality alone. In the beginning, alongside our own universe which encompasses our physical reality and all our spiritual spheres, were created innumerable realities, each within their own physical and energetic world. Like the inside of an orange, these countless realities sit within six distinct segments, contained within the outer skin which is Gods energy, which our minds cannot pierce. Our physical universe and spirit world are within one tiny piece or vesicle within just one segment of the orange, surrounded by innumerable other vesicles.

Each of the segments houses countless other realities. Within just a few of those vesicles are universes that house other sentient life forms. In our segment there are only two realities, or vesicles that have such life forms, including our own.

Each of the segments has boundaries but is part of the same whole. Our immense universe, both the physical and the energetic worlds, all we can see with our deepest space telescopes, is but one small tiny vesicle in the fruit of God's labours. The pith that separates, defines and contains these layers of reality and existence is the energy of God.

All of life has a purpose

Just in the same way that the purpose of our physical life is to provide a vehicle for the soul, through which it might evolve to a position where it is fully realised in its spiritual form, so the purpose of the countless realities and universes within them is to create a habitat that will provide a home for each sentient life form, a habitat that allows them to develop to a point where they are elevated in their spiritual progress.

Once the sentient beings in any given universe have established a common understanding, a mature viewpoint and their primary concern becomes spiritual development, they will come to understand that their differences are merely a reflection of life's diversity, nothing less, nothing more.

Eventually, in the development of the human race, all individuals will reach a point where there is a shared common understanding. All religions, at this point, will effectively come into one, because we have all understood the common bond we share, both physically and spiritually. At this point, when we recognise the enormity of life and the true nature of our role within it, our shared origins and journey, we will be ready to merge with the other six universes.

Every waking moment is a lesson in our development and life will constantly provide us with challenges we have consciously chosen to overcome. These may sometimes feel beyond our ability to surmount. Yet, what feels like a daunting challenge may, in retrospect make us stronger and provide us with what we need to grow. Whatever makes us go beyond what we feel are the limits of our mental and emotional resources can be the next step upwards in our spiritual progression. For if we are able to face times of turmoil and take the lesson they offer us, we have already grown.

Therefore our spiritual evolution is not a hypothetical exercise or an academic theory, but a very real opportunity for advancement that only we are able to fulfil, through the choices we make and the resultant directions we take.

As we progress, so our souls will occupy different levels at different times, according to the degree of learning we have achieved. The higher we go, the harder the lessons we will need to endure to achieve the next level we are aiming for. Yet, once we have learned, we do not need to go through those same lessons again and we can recognise the benefit of having persisted through our periods of greatest growth.

Our limited perspective

The demands of maintaining our existence, gaining physical nourishment and overcoming our challenges mean we need, of necessity, to live in linear time, to be able to face a sometimes uncertain future and triumph. By contrast, in spirit world, we have no real need of time. There, our existence is non-physical and we do not need to perceive a beginning or an end to aid us in our realisations. Yet, the limitations of our spiritual forms, while they are developing, prevent us from ascending to the height that God occupies where everything merely 'is.' For His mind encompasses the whole of time without beginning or end, knowing the fate of every single one of us. We are nowhere near His level of conscious existence where, merely by turning His attention, He can understand the journey of every single leaf, tree, animal and human soul on the planet.

When we contemplate or try to relate to the spiritual universe, we do so from a limited perspective. The human race is still endeavouring to understand our physical universe. Even though we exist within it and it supports us, many of us do not understand the most very basic and immediate elements in our existence, such as why clouds exist, or why the sky is blue, nor can we understand the physics involved in something we can witness every day, such as a sunrise. So, how much harder is it to comprehend that which we cannot physically apprehend.

However, wherever we are on the planet and whatever our situation, although we may not understand the physics of it, we can all appreciate the beauty of a new day. Our relationship with God can be much like our relationship with the sky. From a distance, we see it as blue, but up close, the air is not blue, it is transparent. By the same token, we exist in His domain and up close, when embroiled in the immediacy of our day-to-day lives, we may not be aware of His presence. Yet, when we think of the bigger picture, we are able to perceive His Hand in everything. Having an open mind is a pre-requisite to feeling His presence in our lives and deepening our understanding. By taking a mental step backwards and allowing ourselves to contemplate the possibility of a universal plan, we are more receptive to the force at work behind the scenes and all around us.

Still, it does not follow that by opening our minds we instantly find God. We do not even fully understand our own minds, nor are we fully conversant with our emotions, for all of us can suddenly be surprised by our feelings. We do not control when we feel anger or joy, rather they arise unbidden in reaction to life. We do not even know what happens to our consciousness when we sleep, because one minute we are 'here' and the next we are waking up with no memory of what happened in the meantime, with the exception of dreams we might recall. Bearing in mind we do not know ourselves fully, then how much more difficult is it for us to understand something so immense that it created not only our physical universe but our immortal souls. In perceiving God, we are far more limited than even an ant is in discerning a human being. At least the ant inhabits the same physical world as the human, while God is a being of energy that has manifested our denser realm. Our intelligence and perspective is so much more limited than His, that it is like we are a grain of sand seeking to comprehend a vast beach. All we are conscious of is the sand around us; we may never even see the ocean or that which is beyond our very limited horizon.

Time does not exist merely as we perceive it, as a linear procession of events, those that we are living in now, those that come before and those that are yet to come. While that is what we see, God's perception and perspective encompasses the full extent of time and we merely walk a narrow pathway along it. So it is, with this all embracing knowledge, a seemingly short time to His perception, might be a billion years to our understanding, existing as we do, within physical reality and its limitations. While our soul, the continuing spiritual element of our existence, has eternal life, each physical lifetime is merely a stepping-stone on our pathway of development. As physical beings, subject to the polarities of the universe, we remain encased in perceptions of up and down and past and present. We live in a capsule of time and space, bounded by the immediacy of our surroundings, perceiving night and day as defining factors of our natural lifecycle, while God exists in a limitless eternal form as the Creator of All.

As our journey on Earth continues, humanity will reach a stage where we are ready to hold a common understanding of what spirituality entails. We will then be ready to dispense with the cultural and religious boundaries we have constructed and can then begin to meet our spiritual needs through a singular awareness that encompasses all our similarities and recognises all our differences. When people are able to look at life from a truly spiritual viewpoint, the individual differences between religions becomes less important because the spiritual pathway is recognised as the overreaching reason for our being here. For it is not so important that we find God as it is that we attain a spiritual perspective and incorporate it in our lives so that we might progress.

Eventually our journey of physical life here in this universe will end and no more physical human life forms will populate it. This ending of the human race will come at a time when we have dispensed with the need to have a physical human form and we will no longer require this type of body.

When the human race has matured to this point, where our physical universe no longer serves a purpose, the five original souls who remain with God will have achieved their original purpose of using a physical existence to further their spiritual enlightenment. All the while, our spiritual home in God's Heaven will continue eternally.

Disease

Our journey is one of increasing realisation and the resultant enlightenment is, in itself, the truest healing we can experience. Yet, we experience disease as a necessary part of our journey and as we know from scientific research, disease has many causes, there are physical, genetic and environmental causes and our knowledge of these is expanding daily.

Some people see disease as a form of punishment for our actions here on Earth or make the mistake of assuming disease is divine retribution or a test. The causes of disease are virtually limitless, from athlete's foot to cancer and while the suffering we endure may hold a spiritual lesson for us, we should not confuse a disease or disability as a punishment, rather they are a sad reflection of the chances we take merely by owning a physical body.

This pragmatic overview is one side of the coin, yet for some, disease may be something that is chosen to serve a spiritual purpose or to be endured as a definitive test of inner strength. Because disease can be unpleasant, inconvenient, painful and hard, it is our nature to see it as something imposed from the outside without considering the lesson we can learn from it and an individual who is enduring disease can help others who wish to play a role in caring, to provide those who are scientifically exploring the opportunity to exercise their skills and also to further our understanding of physical existence and of the make-up of our bodies. So while disease from our viewpoint is unwanted, there are many perspectives we can take that show us what opportunities for positive change and development its presence creates.

Our spiritual journey can help us to enhance our day-to-day lives even in the face of illness. It can help us deal with its harsher aspects when we are unwell or perhaps even facing the end of our lives, for while we may escape serious disease in this lifetime, death is something that ultimately confronts us all and there is no escape from this cycle.

Therefore a spiritual pathway, one that opens us to a greater understanding of the cycle of life and death, can help alleviate those aspects of life that are emotionally painful and those that are physically challenging too.

Specific spiritual practices, such as healing meditations, help bring the right energy to our bodies to help us cope, alleviate or effectively combat whatever it is that afflicts us. Some believe that in this way, alongside the healing of our emotions and while elevating our energy levels, a true physical healing can be achieved.

Sadly, the creation of a wondrous and immense physical universe brought with it the possibility of disease. For everything that exists which is good offers the opportunity for the bad to come with it and all ultimately serve a purpose. So, spiritual practices such as meditation connect us with positive energies and those that promote well-being in our thoughts can help us avoid being run down and susceptible to ill health, while widening our viewpoint of life can help us to confront and accept its harsher realities and to be happier, despite whatever physical ailments we own.

When we are facing medical problems then, alongside conventional medicine, we can use every element of our spiritual being to bring ourselves to good health, mentally and emotionally, while perhaps having a profound effect on our spiritual understanding.

However, it is a mistake to feel that we can escape every ailment, for while we can work tirelessly to heal, sometimes it can be our time to experience whatever ill health afflicts us. Therefore, one of the best things we can do for ourselves is to look after our physical body as well as we are able, as it is the vehicle that carries the soul on its journey. For many of us, in this day and age, are pursuing the pleasures our body can bring to the extreme. Indulgences which might otherwise be simple pleasures, such as eating and drinking, can be taken to the extent that they are detrimental to our health.

So, while we might want it otherwise, every element of life we experience opens the doorway to both good and bad. The existence of organic matter allows organisms to grow and feed, no matter what their nature. Bacteria is created, which is the basis of both life and decay, viruses test us and strengthen our body's ability to resist. Even we prey on life forms so that we might prosper and flourish. Within a universe where the imperative is to grow, every form of organism seeks to establish itself and thrive. Where these organisms intrude on us, or where we are unable to provide for our own needs, we experience disease. So, everything has a right to live here, but that means we can experience disease when we fall out of balance. Disease in its extreme can manifest as cancer, a form of anti-life that, once it affects a cell in our bodies, performs much like a black hole in outer space. It is a physical negative element and an example of how we embody the wider spiritual universe, a growth that is unwanted and has only a negative impact, yet exists in many forms. Cancer and black holes destroy their environments, devouring until they eradicate all the matter accessible to them. A perfect world is not viable for us, as we are not yet perfect people. All of us take our chances in life, because here we are in a physical environment, while in spirit world, God has created a world of energetic matter that conforms to His divine will. Here we have both free will and the results of it; those that we experience as positives and those that we have to learn to live with.

Chapter Seven - The Future

Before long, and as we are already beginning to experience, the growing population on the planet will mean increased competition for natural resources. The human race may be driven by hunger, desperation and the need for survival, into acts of self-preservation that set one against the other, causing conflict and even violence.

This conflict means there will be a need for older souls, those that have progressed far enough, to come down here and fulfil roles of mediation and wisdom, guiding the human race to better ways of dealing with its problems.

With this environmental pressure will come a process of separation. Those who are prepared to sacrifice others, to take what is not theirs, to be the originators of violence, will be on one side. On the other will be those who are willing to look at life from a spiritual perspective. It is they who will create a positive way forward for humanity, but they will be thrown into conflict with those who are violent, causing the spiritually minded to need to escape. So people will be thrown into groups where they can escape or embrace the conflict and their motivations will be that much more apparent.

Those who are motivated to survive for the sake of a better life for themselves and others, recognising that there is the need for equality and progress that does not sacrifice those around them, they will form one side of the equation. On the other, we will see those who will do whatever it takes and sacrifice whoever they see fit, to achieve a better life for themselves. Yet because life will be reduced to its most basic because of just this approach to living on the planet, those who are barbaric at heart will reveal themselves that much more readily because they are easier to spot. So life's exigencies will, as ever, bring our inner natures to the surface.

Today when we act, no one may necessarily see the results of what we do, our actions hidden within financial dealings or masked from view, known only by those who experience the results.

In the far flung future, when we are competing for food, for water and for enough space to live, what we do will be that much more evident. Instead of cheating and it being hidden within our financial records, we will be known for whether we take what is not ours. Whether we steal a plate of food will be seen and whether we give out of kindness will be readily apparent.

This cycle has happened on our planet before. Yet, with our new technologies, the next phase may be easier to bear and as the population reduces, we have a choice. We can choose to apply ourselves to life in a way that recognises everyone as equal, we can treat the planet respectfully, or we can seek to carve out as much for ourselves as we are able, regardless of the consequences for everyone else. What we choose will define each of us individually, as much as it will decide the fate of the Earth.

Relationships, our culture and the effect society has on our lives

Just as our family background and the way we are brought up can have a profound effect on the direction our lives take, so the culture we are born into can also have a profound effect, not only on the direction of life, but also on the viewpoints and attitudes we hold. For many of us, our beliefs and attitudes are absorbed from those around us and the common understanding and perspective our culture holds can go a long way towards defining what we think. So we may grow up to adopt the ingrained habits of our upbringing and the society that surrounds us and if we are born into an area of society where violence is accepted as a way of dealing with problems, it might seem natural for us to adopt aggression as a way of life.

Yet, we may be the type of person who is willing to challenge commonly held beliefs, to think independently, to question whether the accepted way of approaching problems is the only way.

For we can find ourselves here on Earth to be actors on a stage, adopting the habits of our youth and acting out our roles without taking an independent viewpoint and applying our insight.

On a spiritual pathway, our inner-calling can lead us to question. We may find ourselves asking whether what is going on in the world around us is in accord with what we would like to see. We may also question the commonly held beliefs, the opinions and the attitudes of ourselves and those around us. For a spiritual outlook should at the very least help us to find ourselves, to find out why we think what we think and why we feel what we feel.

Self-illumination grows with increased awareness and can help shed light on our views and attitudes. We may find that our ingrained assumptions do not have any sound grounding in fact.   For instance, we may have been brought up to think of ourselves as nothing special, as a person with nothing unique about us, or perhaps nothing to offer. By opening our mind through spirituality, we can find that there is absolutely no basis for this negative viewpoint, because each of us is unique and we all serve a purpose. The very act of pursuing a spiritual path can help us become stronger and more independent, as well as a more loving caring and attentive person, because our insight leads us to a greater understanding of the human condition.

By taking a spiritual perspective, we can gain a greater understanding of the difference between the opinions we merely pick up along the way and our truly held beliefs, born out of the wisdom of experience. For we are not here to impose our will, ultimately we are here to learn from what comes to us and it is what we discover through direct comprehension that is of the greatest significance.

What we are told can be at direct odds with what we know to be true. The news and media, while they are here to provide information, are equally interested in exciting our interest and some in their profession can stoop low to achieve the high rewards they desire. We are, each of us, the ultimate decision makers of what we choose to believe, where we choose to focus our interest and how much importance we place on the negative and superficial. We can learn to ignore the sensationalist, not to take on board the superficial, nor to focus on violence, cynicism and lust. For there are many, much more important things we can bring into our lives.

Love can be the most beneficial force there is and here, we are each of us ultimately seeking a love that equals that which is available to us in spirit world. It may be we do not agree or don't care to admit it to ourselves. If either is the case and we have pushed what is the most beneficial force in the universe aside or allowed it to be demoted in our priorities, then we should ask ourselves 'why?' For, if we are not allowing the feeling of love into our lives, we are depriving ourselves of one of the most nurturing, sustaining forces in our universe.

Each of us is born into this life with a purpose which differs from person to person. It may be a seemingly grand mission we are on, such as leading the nation or it can be one of the most valuable things of all, such as setting examples for future generations through the way we choose to live our life.

Despite the spirit world being a place of love, there are still areas on the other side where, due to our actions, we can dwell in loneliness or without feelings of warmth. So, if we have come from a lonely place on the other side, then when we are born here we will be all the more desperate to find fulfilment through love itself. Yet no matter what love we find, it cannot last here in physical life for the eternity that we hope for. The only truly everlasting love comes from a spiritual source, for it is only the love of God and of those who occupy the higher realms of spiritual existence that are constant and will never die. All other forms of love are limited by the length of our physical existence or the limitations of our human emotions. Seek yourself and you will find love. Seek love and you will find yourself.

The Garden of Eden

Our visit to the Garden of Eden starts in the same manner as our visit to the Hall of Learning. Sit comfortably; take some time to relax and allow your body and mind to settle. Feel your breathing become steady and allow all your cares and concerns to fade away. In your mind's eye, visualise your feet standing in a hallway on thick red carpet. Look up and you will see ahead of you an elevator doorway set into a wall in front of you.

The elevator has brass doors and inside it too has carpet that is deep crimson in colour. Stepping inside, directly in front of you is an oblong brass panel with one button at the very top of it and one at the bottom. You press the very top button and the elevator begins to climb to the very top level. Watch the lights above the door as the elevator climbs up each of the levels in sequence. You reach your level, the elevator comes to a halt and you watch as the doors slide smoothly open.

Looking to your left you can see the corridor that leads to the enormous set of double doors with the history of the entire world carved upon them.

Across from you is the ticket man in his tiny glass walled room. You can see him through an open single doorway, sitting at his table. He will recognise you but you do not go towards him, instead you turn right and, ahead of you, down the hallway, is a throne fashioned in solid mahogany, its covering a deep carmine red studded with gold that is at the top of two steps. To your right as you look at the throne is a single doorway with a light shining out of it which leads to the library.

Stepping up to the throne we look behind it and there is a huge deep plum-red velvet draped curtain that hangs from way above us, right the way down to the floor. Stood with the curtain in front of us we part its heavy drapes. Immediately before us is the entrance to a beautiful garden festooned with colourful plants and inhabited by all the animals of every description that have ever lived. Every flower and plant, all living flora and every extinct specimen exists within this garden, alongside every living species of animal on the planet from time immemorial.

We go through the curtain and allow it to fall closed behind us as we step forwards onto a pathway cut into the forest floor.

This is the very definition of paradise. In front of us is an awe-inspiring tropical forest in which you are immediately immersed. You can feel the energy washing over you as you absorb a monumental display of the most colourful tropical plants. All the colours of the rainbow are before you, leaves and fronds, in every shade of green and many colours besides, some sparkling and shining as if freshly rained upon. Enormous flowers, blooms with a soft velvety texture that impress themselves upon you as they peek from every area of the forest you are now surrounded by. Everywhere, each plant is shown at its very best and as you peer through the forest you see endless variety, as though you are peering into paradise, with layer upon layer of vistas stretching out before you, a wall of dazzling colour. In the trees, birds of paradise with fantastical plumage put on a show so magnificent it almost seems unreal.

Wherever we look, we see beauty, beautiful and amazing colours, the vibrancy of the natural world in its most perfect forms, radiating life. Closing our eyes we would still be aware of the sensations around us, the amazing smells, the very air suffused with fragrant perfumes that are life enhancing and make you wish to fill your lungs. The subtle smell of vibrant growth, wafts of vapour heavy with the immediacy of so much perfection. Too much for us to take in. Exotic fungi almost too fantastical to imagine, growing in shapes and sizes we find almost unimaginable. The woody boles of trees meeting earth so rich it supports the luxuriant growth that fills the landscape.

Animals move throughout. Monkeys and lemurs skipping from branch to branch, peering from behind tree trunks as in the distance, the stately progress of elephants through wooded glades moves your eyes to the side and you see giraffes grazing the tree tops, as tiny voles run through fallen leaves and toads and frogs leap. Further off, a waterfall, mountains in the distance and a sky overhead that is far deeper than any you have previously stood under.

Before you a unicorn, no bigger than a Shetland pony, steps up to nuzzle your hand. You must be careful not to touch the unicorn's horn, instead we must move to its tail and allow it to lead us through the tropical paradise around us. As you proceed, every single living creature that has walked the Earth moves in the landscape around you. Moles, birds, everything within creation is there surrounding you as you make your way through lush vegetation. The feeling of harmony is beautiful and everywhere the air is suffused with peace under a sky of the most beautiful blue. As you move forward, in your mind you hear a beautiful melodious sound, so wistful and stirring that it is beyond physical replication, like nothing you have ever heard before, nor will hear elsewhere. So all-pervading is the vibration that it is like a physical presence within you. As you walk along a curve in the path, ahead of you is a clearing and within it a large pool, at the head of which is a wonderful waterfall that falls like a wall of silvern silk into the water below. In the distance are white snow-capped mountains. In the centre of the pool you see the silhouette of a figure, a beautiful woman with her back towards you, waist-deep in the water, combing jet black hair that falls past her waist and spreads out on the surface of the pool in the shape of a fan.

Removing your clothes, you neatly fold and lay them on the ground beside you. Stepping forwards, you slowly walk into the inviting presence of the water. As it touches your skin, you can feel it is invigorating and as smooth and soft as silk.

The woman does not acknowledge your presence. Instead, with her eyes averted and her back still turned, she continues to comb the length of her ebony locks, each strand clearly defined and stretched out like a ribbon of polished ebony as she tends to it.

As you move forwards, you naturally reach a depth where the water envelopes you and you proceed in a smooth and graceful breast stroke, getting closer and closer to the waterfall before you.

As you reach the waterfall, you find you can stand once more, waist deep in the pool, planting yourself on the soft sand at the bottom of the deluge, feeling the soles of your feet grounded and your toes aware of each granule of sand. Before you, three solid stone steps lead upwards to the very base of the waterfall. Stepping forwards, you rise from the pool until you are directly underneath the falling water. In one fluid motion, you raise your arms and open them to form the shape of a Y, fanning out your fingers and stretching your palms wide. Taking a step forwards, you are engulfed by the beautiful flood that falls upon you like a deluge of soft rain, full of shimmering stars and rainbows as the light catches each droplet.

Looking upwards, you can see the sky and the source of the waterfall overhead, glimpsed through a fountain of life giving essence, millions of droplets that rush towards you, covering you without the sensation of pressure and cleansing every inch of your being.

Taking your time, you stand immersed in the silvery spray for as long as you wish, allowing it to envelop you and saturate as it runs over your entire body. You feel it wash over you, a rainbow of light, striking your hands with a gentle flow, over your head and eyes and running down your arms caressing your skin as it runs down to your feet, the droplets bouncing down the stone steps and leaping to merge with the pool. Each moment of immersion cleanses you and fills you with energy, leaving your skin with a satiny glow.

When you are ready, you turn away from the waterfall and step down into the pool, allowing the water to support you as you immerse yourself in its embrace, submerging yourself once more. Moving gracefully through the water, you pass the lady with the ebony hair, her back still turned and step smoothly and silently from the pool.

Finding your clothes where you left them, you dress and feeling exhilarated and alive, find the unicorn patiently waiting for you at the water's edge. Taking its tail, you follow it along the path, walking through the tropical paradise as you retrace your steps.

Eventually you find yourself at the curtains and, allowing its tail to fall gently from your hand, give your thanks to the unicorn for acting as your guide. Saying your farewells, you pull the curtains apart and let them drop behind you as you walk forwards.

Ahead of you is the high backed throne. Stepping around it and down the steps you leave the garden behind you and walk down the corridor to return to the lift.

Pushing the button in the wall, the lift doors slide smoothly open and you step in. Allowing the door to shut behind you, you press the bottom button on the brass panel and then descend once more until you arrive to the level from which you started. Stepping out onto the red carpet, you focus on your feet, allow your mind to return to behind your eyelids, bring your consciousness to the room from which you originally started and allow yourself to return from your meditation.

Chapter Eight - Religion and Spirituality

There is much debate as to the nature of religion and spirituality. The difference between the observance of a spiritual code and an active spiritual quest can be difficult to identify from the outside and the extreme lengths that people go to in the name of religion are one of the most hotly debated topics of modern times.

The point of a spiritual quest is to increase our understanding of ourselves, to lead ourselves to a better mental state, to understand humanity, the bigger picture of the spiritual universe and why we are here. It is a personal exploration of everything we know, to find that which we do not. To achieve this, our mind needs to open, to embrace and appreciate everything that is around us and everything we have within ourselves. This appreciation cannot be achieved with a narrow-minded approach, for, by its very nature, a narrow-mind opposes a spiritual appreciation of life. Nor is an angry or destructive viewpoint going to serve our spiritual awakening, for to have a mind-set that wishes to destroy or is overcome with negativity, we necessarily have to switch ourselves off and accustom ourselves to the suffering of others, when in fact, to pursue a spiritual pathway, we must be alive to the feelings of those we encounter and aware of the impact our actions can have upon them. Therefore, our pathway cannot be destructive, for if it is, it cannot be spiritual. Yet many people will carry out extreme acts in the name of religion, ignoring what impact their actions can have on themselves and other people.

Religion can have many positive aspects and many cultural roles it fulfils, acting as a cohesive force in communities and providing us with the regularity of a calendar of events that recognise important times and give structure and communality of purpose to daily lives. While these can be very positive, none of these aspects are necessarily, in themselves alone, spiritual ones. A spiritual journey is an inner quest for peace of mind. Ultimately, it can only be successful to the extent we are willing to care for others and observe positive habits, so it will have guidelines we need follow. However it is very important that we are honest with ourselves and deal with the emotions and feelings that hold us back. So we need to loosen the intellectual barriers that stop us recognising that there could be more to life and allow us to reach out to that which is greater than ourselves. If our religion enables us to do all of these things, then we know we are on a spiritual pathway, but if we are using our religion as a way of reinforcing our own preconceptions and perhaps in a way that leads us to extreme behaviours, it is in fact leading us away from our spiritual goal.

Our religion should be serving a spiritual purpose and leading us to a more complete and fulfilled existence. Likewise, if we adopt any spiritual pathway, then it will have religious aspects within it. There will be observances, prayers, meditations or physical postures we adopt and practice. There will be aspects of the spiritual universe we tune into and interpret. All these things can build into a structure and belief that serves as our religion. The negative sides of religion, therefore, have nothing to do with our spiritual pathway and everything to do with human nature. Also, while we associate religion with reaching out for a higher source, and at the same time, an inner life, there are many things we can worship religiously, be it money, sex, work, sport, celebrity or politics. Any of these things can become our main preoccupation and the goal we seek to achieve with our lives. It is human nature to seek things that stimulate us and prioritise them above all others and sometimes to our own detriment. So, whatever our religion, be it consciously chosen or not, only we will know if we are following it to enlightenment or taking a pathway that limits us, or allows our ignorance to hold sway.

All religious pathways are a search for something higher than ourselves so that we might find a higher purpose within ourselves. We may follow a book, a man, or a group, yet ultimately each of us is seeking to 'know,' to find a way of life that is suitable, that gives us purpose and to find our own version of happiness. Yet wherever we seek it, happiness is ultimately contained in our attitude more than it is in the things that surround us. If we achieve our spiritual goals, we can reach a point of no turning back; we enter a state of knowing, where our entire existence is put into perspective and our inner self is paramount. For, once we have paid the price of gaining this knowledge, through living a life that teaches us what is important within it, we have gained a wider consciousness more a part of us than our physical life.

Whether it be self-development, spirituality or a religion that leads us, any of these routes can have practices which aid in achieving a state of increased awareness. Many of them can lead us to a point where we suspect that there is more to life, but it is only our personal experience that will prove it beyond a shadow of a doubt.

There is enough proof available, no matter what pathway we follow. Any direct encounter with the spiritual universe, be it with God, with those who have passed over, or through our clairvoyant senses, each of these can provide us with irrefutable personal proof that confirms this knowledge within us.

As we are schooled by our chosen religion, so should we be with everyone, without exception. As we treat ourselves, so we should treat others, with kindness and love, while we cherish what life offers. The tenets of love apply to everyone and no religious observances should exclude others from this community, for we are all ultimately equal, placed on this Earth to develop and grow.

Everything we do on the spiritual pathway requires authenticity and honesty; we must practice what we preach if we are to have credibility with ourselves, set examples and allow others to observe what works and what does not.

While we are not subordinate to anyone or anything, there is a structure and a framework to the universe that we work within. Just as gravity dictates the pull Earthward, so our actions have cause and effect and there are great forces at work in the universe, to which by comparison, we are mere grains of sand. A spiritual outlook alerts us to the signs that we might otherwise overlook or see as coincidences. Eventually we can recognise that there is significance in every element and every occurrence in the universe.

On our spiritual pathway we can also recognise just how significant our life is and how precious, as well as just how small we are when compared to the ultimate source of Creation. Therefore, we must be prepared to stand up and be accountable for our actions just as much as we should be prepared to revere that which is greater than all of us.

Whatever our religion, whatever our aspiration, an essential element will always be giving up some part of ourselves to a greater good. Recognising our connection with this bigger picture is a step towards allowing life to flow without unnecessary interference. While we have our own free will and we are here to express it, much of the worry we put into life is superfluous. The act of letting go can allow our lives to proceed without the excessive over-thinking that serves no purpose. In prostrating ourselves to God, we are offering our good wishes to the universe. By connecting with the universal energy, we naturally learn to let go and take life in our stride far more than if we believed that the physical is all there is.

This ability to let go of our thought patterns, our over-thinking and our preconceptions is key to allowing our clear vision to develop. For the clearer our mind is of our own agenda, the easier it is to interpret the information we are all able to receive from outside our own minds. So our clear vision, our healing faculties and our emotions all function so much better if we are able to simply 'let go and let it be'.

By letting go, we are able to progress spiritually and as a natural result, we are increasingly conscious of the lessons we receive from life.   Worrisome or troubling situations can become valuable instructions for our own development because, by learning not to focus on an instinctive reaction and rather seeking to find the lesson we can learn, we will find a more positive outcome.   In this way, those situations that might otherwise seem too hard to bear can be seen in perspective and we can recognise how they serve to teach us about our own lives.   Letting go of the rubbish in our minds leaves us free of the false notion that we are in control of that which we are not, allows us to receive another's perspective, to entertain spiritual notions and allow for other points of view. Most importantly, we can see our own responses for what they are and, over time, this enables us to develop as human beings.   For only through experience is wisdom learned.

The independence of thought we gain from a spiritual perspective means we can recognise exactly what we are responsible to in life. For those of us who are of a sensitive nature, it shows where we are falsely trying to please others. For those of us who are wedded to our own thoughts and ideas, it shows us how other points of view can be valid.   For those of us who feel lost and are looking for answers, it shows us that we have our own inner ability to find them. Whatever our nature, our problems or our worries, learning to keep our mind open can help free us from our own prejudices and limitations and, ironically, allows us to be that much more true to ourselves.   This then helps us to be that much more authentic as people, being accountable for our actions, what we say and do and even responsible for our thought patterns.   We gain far greater clarity of emotion and even a greater love for ourselves. As a result, our lives naturally become less complicated and we are able to go with the flow as we develop true self-belief.

This change isn't necessarily something that happens overnight, rather we learn, over time, to live in accordance with our Higher Self and listen to its truth, letting go, opening up and looking beyond.

Taking a spiritual approach doesn't necessarily mean that we are here to put everyone else first, but it does mean that we, at the very least, learn to consider them as human beings. The best approach is to do unto others as you would have them do unto you, nothing more demanding nor difficult than that and yet so many of us find reason to ignore this most basic and logical of tenets.

Our spiritual journey can be as simple or demanding as we choose. It is our inner conscience that tells us how high we feel we need to go or how much priority our spiritual journey has in our lives. For many, it is merely right to be the best person we can be, while for a few, it is a journey of constant discovery and growth.

Clairvoyance and our spiritual progression

If a person chooses to pursue a spiritual pathway, they are engaged in a search. They may be looking to know who they are, understand life's purpose, find personal enlightenment, attain greater inner contentment, or love others unconditionally and achieve peace of mind. Whatever personal search, religion or spiritual path we adopt is our choice. What is important is that we find what feels right for us.

The pathway outlined in this book is one that is communicated directly from the world of spirit and therefore has one particular emphasis; developing our understanding so that we may perceive the world in a much wider context. In this way, we can prepare ourselves to recognise spiritual phenomena and begin to appreciate the world of energy in which our soul resides.

Our spiritual life is paramount if we are to achieve lasting happiness and the psychic gifts we all possess are the ideal way of achieving this goal, for they allow us to directly perceive the spiritual universe for ourselves.

Spirituality is a journey of the mind and the soul combined. Whatever your religion, it should allow you the personal freedom to find your way forward, the tools to develop yourself and a way of understanding what life offers and your purpose within it.

There are many ways to achieve peace of mind and the reason personal enlightenment is so important is that it offers you the greatest chance of achieving this for yourself. We are all part of the energy of the universe, the light, the source where we all belong and of which we are all part. Whatever pathway you choose towards happiness, it should offer you the opportunity to live in love and offer it to others without judgement or restriction.

Spirituality and many religions offer us a singular purpose, a pathway that, if followed, can lead each individual to their own personal enlightenment. There is also the prospect of being part of a collective thought pattern that is conducive to peace on Earth. Whatever route we choose, it should offer goodness and self-knowledge without harming one another and the opportunity to learn the purpose of life and its creation.

Whatever pathway we progress on, the practice of unconditional love and compassion can lead the practitioner to enlightenment and when you find it, it enhances everything about you and brings increased freedom from worries and doubts.

The perspective we offer in this book recognises both God and rebirth. From this recognition comes a faith that places an emphasis on the value and meaning of each and every life we live, that what you give out is given back to you twofold and that personal growth gives us the freedom to live well, leading us to enlightenment and a permanent place in God's Heaven.

Fulfilling our karma means we can find liberation and eventually our permanent place in spirit world. Our tasks in life can be hard and if we are taking a spiritual approach, we must learn not to be too hard on ourselves. Our physical journey is quite simple in that we will be born and we will pass over at the end of our days. God asks nothing of us other than that we are good to each other and to ourselves, that we multiply, flourish, respect the planet and be accountable for our actions.

Yet we have choices and enlightenment comes in greater or lesser degrees according to the deeds we do and the lives we live. We cannot merely think or meditate ourselves into enlightenment. It comes to us as a result of practicing what we preach and being true to ourselves in how we act, think and feel. Ultimate enlightenment is a result of countless smaller realisations, many mini-enlightenments that build up a picture so that we recognise ourselves, our purpose and our place in life. Therefore the essence of enlightenment is understanding and with it comes the ability to feel a sense of total belonging as we take our natural place in the universe.

Our personal insight can clear as we pursue our pathway and aid us in our search for enlightenment, in that it provides us with an unencumbered perspective that aids us in recognising our place in the spiritual universe, the value of life and the results of our actions. It helps us to understand ourselves, our emotional reactions and the reasons we are here. Therefore, developing the psychic gifts we are born with can directly aid us in our search for enlightenment.

To God, we are young children, so bad behaviour is not unexpected. Learning our thoughts and feelings and how they are affected by what we do is an essential part of our journey. For we are His creation, both the soul and the human lives we live and, as with any good Father, He is there if we need Him. However, we have freedom of will and in every respect it is up to us what we do. In God's eyes we do not have to work hard to find him, for when we pass over we will exist in His realm and will know through the very existence of our soul that there is a spiritual life after death. So while we may pursue spiritual development in any number of ways, God will not judge us for the manner in which we seek, provided it is with a wish to better ourselves and in a way that we help one another. He is not there to criticise or judge and it is for each of us to find the pathway that is right for us. Therefore, no more is demanded of us than what we are able to give. Our Higher Self manifesting as our conscience will tell us whether we are putting our all into life and doing the best we can. It is up to us to be honest with ourselves and make the most of every opportunity.

The reasons we choose a spiritual pathway are diverse. Many take up a religion as a way of escaping life. If this is the case, then at some stage we will need to come back to down to Earth and relate to our position within humanity. For only by taking part can we help people. It is by interacting with our fellow human beings that we are able to test whether what we are doing is right. We need to check that we are not merely pursuing a spiritual path as a means of escaping responsibility. If we do not consider others and our obligation to the human race we are taking ourselves away from enlightenment rather than towards it. We can seek enlightenment through meditation and prayer but if we are not integrating our everyday actions with our goal then we are deluding ourselves. Ultimate enlightenment is only ours if we learn to put other people first.

You do not need to adopt any special way of acting to show you are of a spiritual leaning. Instead, what is important is what you do and how you act. The reasons we are here are diverse and there are many aspects to the meaning of life. Religions may adopt many different codes, modes of dress and ways of expressing ones faith, but what is important is our spiritual journey. In the same way that we can wear a religious garb and be devoid of spirituality, so equally we can give no outward sign of our thoughts but still be incredibly spiritually advanced. Therefore, religious codes are only important in what they do for us spiritually. Our religion may show us how to become humble in that we don't try to make ourselves different for the notice we receive, or it may be that we need to learn brotherhood and our religion brings us together in a community with a common purpose. There are many purposes for religion and positive reasons for it to exist.

Many religions recognise that there is the opportunity of an ultimate enlightenment and to permanently pass beyond physical existence when we leave this life. There is a general recognition that helping one another helps us to further our spiritual goals and some may concentrate on our helping humanity or helping all living beings. We cannot be selfish in our goals, nor can we spend a lifetime helping others and ignoring the spiritual practices that open us up to the bigger picture. Good people become more enlightened all the time, by adopting lives that are good and helping other people without bias as to who we feel is worthy.

We all get the results of our karma, whether we worship God, have faith or no faith at all. If we are being good to one another, God does not worry about what we wear, it is whether we are being true to ourselves and those who are in need that is important.

Getting what we need

When we are most in need, we can quite naturally look to the physical things in life to solve our problems and a spiritual approach isn't necessarily going to provide material solutions. However, it will lead us in the right direction to understand and deal with life, finding what it is we can learn and gain from it.

There are those who believe we can solve our spiritual problems and achieve our material goals through spiritual means. This approach can lead us to request from the spiritual universe a huge sum of money, a new partner who is able to meet our every need, a car, a house or whatever it is we need to meet our physical desires. All these, the thinking goes, may be ours if we wish hard enough for them. The implication is that by focusing our will, we can draw down from the spiritual realm whatever we want and whatever we desire from life can be ours. This is not the case.

Universal energy radiates from that which we call God, the ultimate source of compassion, understanding and unconditional love. Its purpose is to nurture the whole of existence and to further humanity's spiritual advancement. It functions to progress our soul's journey, for it is our soul that is the ultimate receptacle and originator of our spiritual experiences. It functions to sweep our pathway clear of the physical obstructions, emotional worries and the situations that hinder us. It is a very powerful force that can have a hugely positive effect on our journey and especially if we consciously invite it to work with us.

Just as karma has its own natural laws that we cannot effect, so the universal energy has its own structure and rules. It serves to nurture our soul's development, help those who are truly in need, but always solely in a way that is in accordance with God's will and that aids our spiritual progression.

When we are on the other side, we are all part of a collective thought, yet we all have our individual needs. There, in a place without boundaries consisting purely of energy we are potentially limitless. Here on Earth, the material life we are so privileged to possess comes with limitations and threats and the temptation is to focus merely on the immediate. However, there is so much more to life than what we consume and own; look at the immensity of the opportunity that having a physical existence provides. Here, we can enjoy the mere fact that we are alive, experience the exultation of finding our passions and experiencing them through our bodies. Our material existence serves a purpose in feeding our soul with all the myriad possibilities for experience that come through the mere possession of life, but to become focused on the material for its own sake misses the point. The point is to embrace life to the full for whatever it offers at this given moment in time, to enjoy the experience and to share it with family and friends and whoever is around us. Spiritual life focuses on the very essence of what we are and that is not measured in any currency, nor in what life gives us, but rather in what we make of it, setting examples and proving our value to ourselves and others.

Therefore, the universal energy answers when we are desperately calling out for help. Yet it can only bring into our life that which we are ready for at that time. Ultimately, the universal energy comes to us when we are ready to accept it, to the degree we are ready to receive it.

If we are choosing to view life as a spiritual journey we are taking a very wide view in what can be a restrictive environment. By opening our minds to life's greater purpose, for us as individuals and the human race as a whole, we relate to the widest perspective. What we discover within ourselves can be a revelation and everyday life can then, by contrast, seem mundane or limiting. However, if we can understand that everything has a purpose, the act of opening ourselves to the universal energy helps us recognise the significance of everything in our everyday lives and so brings more meaning to them. The universal energy can help us recognise our greatest opportunities for inner freedom. Through interacting with it, we can understand our emotions, that we each have a common link and a shared inner purpose. It can develop us as a human being to that we learn to live our life to the full. Once we understand where true inner fulfilment lies, we can see why the highest expression of everything we do is love.

We live in a technological age where for many of us, physical survival is to a point assured. Many of us know we have our next meal on the table and modern medicine has extended our life span. Whether we recognise it or not, physical life is all about aiding us in bettering ourselves on our spiritual pathway so that we might go beyond what we already are.

The fact that our lifespan is increasing also means that we have that much longer to put right our wrongs and to complete our tasks. Whether our life is one of banquets or scraps, it is how we cope with and react to our situation that determines how we develop and the extent of our spiritual progress.

Negative and positive experiences all have their place and we learn on a spiritual and emotional level through our reactions to those experiences. What we take with us when we pass over is the sum of our total existence down here. Therefore, on the other side we are only able to 'be' and relate to that which we have experienced here. The law of karma means that how we react to our experiences is key. What we give out we get back. If we react negatively, it can hold us back from achieving the emotional and spiritual growth our lessons were meant to guide us to. If we pass over and recognise that our journey on Earth has been wasted, perhaps by having avoided the challenges set before us, imagine how that could feel.

If we have failed to respond positively to what a life has offered us, then our next reincarnation will help us to progress. This is partly why we need to come back. Time and time again, many of us come down to repeat the process of learning, absorbing the necessary lessons; each lifetime offering us the opportunity to achieve that which we set out for. So, the universal energy communicates with our inner-self throughout our everyday lives, offering us a medium through which we can progress on our spiritual journey. It may work to improve the troubling relationships we are experiencing, or attract people into our life who can bring help, friendship, insight and relief from what is interfering with our soul's progression. For our troubles can produce states of mind that are detrimental, even destructive. Calling upon the universal energy can help us with the outside influences that are slowing our journey unnecessarily and standing in the way of our learning. Our physical journey may then benefit because our soul can achieve the goals that were set out for us before we came to Earth. It is not an energy that feeds negativity, selfish desires or material success for its own sake, instead it recognises and responds to our innermost needs.

So the universal energy naturally orders itself into a pattern that can answer a genuine need through the process of human life. The mistake we make is in imagining that merely by visualising all the things we want and projecting that out to the universe, that we will be answered by it providing us with all we desire. The universe follows God's plan, not ours, and when we ask for something, why we are asking and the nature of our motivation is more important than that which we are asking for. So, with any aggravating situation where we are being bullied, subjugated, restricted or held back, we may ask the universe to provide us with help and the means for a way forward. We can also ask for what we need to develop positively. So, a medical researcher may ask for inspiration in finding the next step forward in her scientific endeavours so that the needs of humanity might be met, or a parent might ask for the right guidance for a troubled child. One may find the right teacher coming their way that relates to their child's need and another a grant of money to further their goals, but the answers are not necessarily material and those that are facilitate an authentic and essential need that will bring good to one or many.

When we ask the universal energy for help, it functions like a giant sifting machine, threshing out the wheat from the chaff, separating genuine needs from those requests we make out of desire or desperation for a release from responsibility. We cannot pervert or subvert the universal energy to our will, nor manipulate or recruit it to serve our selfish desires. Our desires are born of weakness, insecurity or even greed and the universal energy wants to help us overcome these facets and not to pander to them.

Human life is frail, vulnerable and short lived and the universal energy sustains us and assists us in fulfilling those wishes that are in accordance with our purpose. If we exclusively seek to prioritise our own desires, then we could be missing out on life's meaning. So we need to de-clutter our minds and allow the energy to work with us, unobstructed by that which is born of selfishness, weakness, greed or desire.

Another function of the universal energy is that it provides balance between humanity and God. There are two very distinct perspectives on human life and its purpose. When viewed from a material perspective, life can seem restricting, for we may feel we never have enough. When viewed from a spiritual perspective, human life is full of beautiful opportunities for growth. Because of the sometimes horrendous challenges we experience, we can lose sight of this and we can fall into the trap of succumbing to our worries and doubts.

All of our requests for help are heard and many are met. However, the universal energy is not here to protect us from physical life, rather it guides and promotes the furtherance of our life's purpose and that may take our entire lifespan to fulfil. As humans we are not constant and our minds can change like the wind. One day's major concerns may not be remembered in a month's time and that which we feel we most desire may later on even come to repulse us. We are here to experience the results of our actions and work through these unfounded fears. Therefore, the universal energy is not flowing to satisfy our whims, because these change with our minds; rather it is the deepest tide, so subtle that the more we let go of our day-to-day concerns, the more we can feel its pull, the tug of its urging to take us in the direction most beneficial to our soul.

By putting our wishes out to the universe, we are raising our anchor and setting our sail; allowing the universal wind to take us in the right direction. By leaving the harbour of our preconceptions, we can get on with our journey. By putting forward a clear message about what we most desire to learn, or achieve, that which we wish to be part of our journey, the winds of the universal energy are then able to steer us. By allowing life to flow rather than fighting to navigate around sometimes imaginary dangers on a course that ultimately takes us nowhere, we instead take a voyage of constant discovery.

The universal shopping list

There is a clear distinction between the physical manifestations that arrive to help us spiritually and wishing for material things in our life for their own sake, yet these distinctions can be very subtle. The ability we all possess, to let go, allowing a natural order to establish itself in our lives and prepare the ground for the right things to come to us, is sometimes mistaken as an ability to indulge in a material shopping spree from the universe's catalogue. We may wish to take short cuts, ignoring the part we play in life, unwilling or unable to make the effort, wishing to remain the same, unchanged and unchanging. If, instead, we wish for help in a direction that fulfils us and provides society with a valuable service, such as embarking on a career as a teacher, policeman, nurse, counsellor, fire-fighter or anyone who helps us live our lives and we do it for the right reasons, then we are far more likely to be in the flow. It is not that the material things or riches are contrary to spirituality, rather the spiritual energy is working on a subtler level and its focus is to further our development, not to increase what we own. Material possessions can serve a positive purpose; it may be that a rich person devotes his or her money to the alleviation of hunger, or that a successful businessman devotes his profits to developing an ethical service. Alternatively, we may guard our money jealously until the bitter end, not caring whom it benefits or harms, but focusing on the power and comfort money brings. Money is neither a positive nor a negative force; it is merely a tool for us to use and is not the focus of the universal energy. The more we know ourselves, the less significance material wealth acquired for its own sake will have in our lives.

A positive attitude can be a very valuable asset. If we trust that life has a purpose and will provide opportunities for fulfilment and reward, then that can lighten our load and give us a chance at true happiness, no matter what our life situation. That is where true fulfilment lies, not hinged on what material success we achieve, but ultimately in the simple act of seeking personal fulfilment, of knowing we are doing our best. What we learn from our journey here is what we take over when we return to spirit world. Therefore, if we can couple a spiritual attitude with a conscious effort to tune into the energy of the universe, we can be fulfilled in a way that transcends what car we drive and whether we get to spend our waking hours in ways that indulge or stimulate. Where we choose to focus and what we place an emphasis on in our lives determines what we take with us into the realms of our spiritual afterlife, where all is energy and the material and physical have no place.

However, spirituality isn't about self-denial, it is natural for us to want respite from life's pressures and to enjoy it. When the going is tough, typically we might wish for escape, perhaps enough riches to ensure that whatever we want can be ours, or 'just enough so we would never have to work again' and not have to endure the strain of having to provide or strive for survival. What we must ask ourselves is why we are asking. The universal energy responds to intent. Our motivation is key when we form our intent and cannot be separated from it. If we are wishing for money, it may be that we want to escape from our daily responsibilities because we find them boring or onerous, therefore our motivation is coloured by a need for escape. We shouldn't feel we are judged for this. Yet it may be our karma to work hard so that we might achieve that which we most desire with a sense of self-fulfilment. Having a windfall or lottery win may therefore actually divert us from fulfilling our karma. Likewise, we may be here to achieve spiritual accomplishments, so life challenges us to bring forth the best from ourselves. If this is the case then, much as we might find life materially challenging, how can God's universal energy respond positively to a request for escape when it is our life's goal to be the best we can be and bring to life the best we can offer it?

This does not mean that we need live lives of hardship or penury, rather it means that we should seek our fulfilment from the good feeling of genuine friendship, of giving, of unconditional love, of helping and caring. 'Ask and you shall receive' is an invitation to bring good feeling into your life.

It may be that we set our mind to something and by visualising an accomplishment and working hard enough to achieve success, the people we work with and those we do business with respond positively and respect our dedication and drive to meet our goals. The spiritual energy would only aide this process if it fulfils a need, making ourselves a better person, helping those in need, stimulating people's lives in a positive way or helping our family and friends. So there are many levels on which our positivity may express itself and be met by life, but a cheque may not fall into our lap merely because we want it.

The spiritual universe is not there to progress our material life, rather our material life is there to inform our spiritual existence. If we have a dream to build something to serve the needs of our community, such as a park or community centre, or wish to help someone in need, then we may put a wish out to the universe that can be answered. However, it may answer us by introducing people into our lives who help us to work towards our goal so that we are fulfilled while we bond with other like-minded souls. So the universal energy may aide us, but we have to make personal effort.

Our karma also plays a role and it can be that we are given an easy route to money. It may be our karma to have things handed to us or to acquire great wealth and how we use it is another part of our journey. It can be squandered, even frittered away, or hoarded and put to no good use. Once we have abundance on any level, it is far more fulfilling to share of what we have rather than to keep it solely for ourselves. A life of luxury delivers nothing of spiritual use to the person who possesses it if they do not use it to help others.

Hard work and altruistic aspirations are the safest routes to acquiring money, because they run less risk of making us greedy, arrogant or close minded. If we are not yet ready for the universal energy to work with our lives in a certain way, we may ask and ask and not be answered.

What is in fact a very simple topic can seem complicated because we attach such significance to our material well-being. Part of our karma is the material wealth we have acquired a relationship with, therefore naturally in any given lifetime we may be here to experience wealth or the lack of it, to have more money than we need or to have just enough to match our needs.

Money can be used in all sorts of ways, for the pursuit of power, to help others, or to help ourselves. Having money can bring all sorts of responsibilities and considerations that we may not have anticipated. Money can isolate us, the motivations of good friends can be doubted as we cannot trust they relate to us for ourselves alone. Likewise, if we spend our money in the hope that it will bring happiness in its own right, we are working with a false hope. For even the rich and famous can have enough money to fulfil supposedly every Earthly desire, but find themselves addicted to drugs or so unhappy that they suffer depression. There is no guarantee that money will bring happiness. Money can work in insidious ways. We may find ourselves befriending people because of what they have, hoping they will provide for us materially, or we may find ourselves thinking less of those who are poorly dressed than those who are expensively attired.

If we focus on developing ourselves spiritually then that can deliver greater peace of mind, regardless of what we own. Then, what others possess becomes less important than who they are as people. We are less likely to judge or measure the value of them on the basis of what they do for us and rather enjoy them for what they are.

Almost everyone on the planet would welcome a life of luxury and ease, but only a few of us would successfully develop spiritually through an easy life. How can the universe sustain all of us in a life of material luxury – who will manufacture the cars or provide the food we want to eat? For the universal energy cannot meet our needs at the cost of others. The same rule applies if we are praying for a bothersome influence to be removed from our life, an unruly neighbour for instance. It may actually be part of our lesson to learn patience or to deal with situations without anger. So we must qualify every prayer, every request with at least an inner recognition that it can happen only 'if it be God's will.' It may not be part of our journey to have a life free of problems, but rather it may be that we are destined to develop through the particular trial we are facing. Self-realisation may be aided by sitting in meditation and guiding ourselves spiritually, but we only develop by living a life that tests us. What we pray to have taken away from us may be that we most need to go through. So, to receive love we must first give it and to learn patience we must experience something beyond our ability to cope.

Money can be a lesson in its own right. Once we have money in quantities that delivers us power, with it can come the ability to influence people's lives for good or ill. Working with others, receiving their good will, all of these things can help us have good feelings in life. Therefore, we only have one shot at life so make your prayers about furthering ambitions for your spiritual goals, to help others, or to help you to develop in a way that is going to be beneficial to society.

Regardless of whether we are seeking money for a spiritual purpose or not, then having a strong intention can work for us, but remember if we are seeking money for its own sake then we will need to consider carefully what we wish for. If it is not our allotted time to receive money beyond our needs, then we may not receive it. If we are wishing for money to help us escape a situation not of our making, then it may fall in our lap, but are we 100% sure that we are ready to leave that situation? We should not focus on having enough money to live on, rather we should focus on living and having enough to give on!

The universal energy is our friend and it delivers what we need when it is most needed. Like a wishing well, we throw in our wish and the ripples it creates radiate out, bringing back that which we most need. Like the tide, it never comes too late, it is a friendly force much larger than are we. Therefore, a prayer to 'please help this sick child' may be answered by any means possible; a person or a healer or doctor who is best suited to their needs may appear, or a family may unite to provide aid. So it is with life where what we wish for may not be the answer to our prayers that we think it is, for enlightenment comes when we meet our needs for inner-fulfilment in a way that matches the needs of the universe.

Prayer

God is the reason behind our lives and all of reality, the originator and source of the Universal energy which radiates from Him to every corner of our universe and beyond. While we may seek answers to our lives by throwing out wishes into His universe, if we are open to the idea of a Creator, with an independent intelligence, we can also approach Him directly for our answers. For if we learn to listen and work with God, it can have a profound effect on our lives. If our mind is sincerely open, then speaking with Him directly and asking for answers through prayer allows our insight to develop as we learn to recognise the subtler messages and lessons His universe is bringing to us. Being open enough to hear and willing to learn from what is going on in our lives means we are far more likely to get from life what we truly need, than if we merely wished for what we most wanted. Therefore, we can go to the universal energy to help bring into our life what we most need, but it is God who can help us by providing answers and insight into the direction we should choose.

In reality then, by way of example, a request for a glossy, fast car, if couched to the universal energy might be rejected and we would never know why. We might do everything correctly, structuring a daily practice of sending out our wish and focusing our intention, but it might never be realised for reasons unknown to us. In the meantime, we would not have developed in any way. By way of contrast, if we have belief and couch the same request to God, if we have learned to listen to him, then He might show us we have some growing up to do. He might put steps in place to help us understand ourselves a little better, perhaps using our wish for a fast car as the starting point in a conversation, so that we might become conscious of what good we could do for ourselves and others instead of wanting something for its own sake.

What should we pray for?

Pray for others to help them in life. Pray for them to be happy. Pray for enough to realise your aspirations. Pray for those things which you have a need for, not for those things that will make your life one of escapism. Pray for assistance in working to help others. Pray for the sick. Pray for the elderly and those who are facing death. Make your family and friends your priority and your own development your focus.

Life should be a journey of gradual progression, one that gives us the opportunity to take in what we learn as we are going along, without having to experience so much that we become overloaded. Prayer is a way of connecting more deeply with ourselves, with God and with our lives so that we become more part of what is going on around us while allowing us to lighten our burdens.

Too much negativity can make our lives flat, as can living so fast that we never get the opportunity for enjoying what is good for us and prayer is a way of slowing things down enough and understanding where negativity originates from, so that we can fully take part in life. Being freer to enjoy the moment allows us to gather precious memories, bonding and sharing good times with others. For our lives are lived in vain if we do not increase the amount of goodness in the world around us.

The three levels of evolution

Not many people actively consider the nature of our reality and approach life from a questioning perspective. Comparatively few of us have an outlook that consistently prioritises the world as a whole, so that it has equal priority to our own needs.

In our soul forms, in spirit world, we are in a far better position to take in how unique and unusual the planet Earth is, than when we are living upon it. Hanging here in space, our world, a great big ball of a planet, sits seemingly unsupported, in the middle of empty nothingness, hosting life that teems upon it and all the while surrounded by billions of other planetary bodies and stars in a reality without limits. Many astronauts have had a personal taste of this perspective, seeing how incredible the planet is, housing billions of souls against a backdrop of emptiness. Many of them report that seeing the globe from afar changed their outlook of humanity, appreciating for the first time that we are one people with a shared home.

So it is that if we consider only our immediate surroundings and influences and cast our thoughts no further, we create a limited human perspective. This then means that we do not consider the bigger picture and purpose of life. It is understandable and very easy for us to get wrapped up in the immediate and it can take a major shock, such as a war or natural disaster, an earthquake or flood, for us to consider our fellow humanity. In the meantime, we spend our days dealing with life's challenges, while we use up the time this body has borrowed for one life. If the physical universe and physical life is more immense than we can comprehend, how much more challenging and mind expanding is it to consider the spiritual universe in which we all dwell?

Street parties used to be the norm in our culture, while now we have problems merely getting along with our neighbours or even knowing who they are. Instead, we buy and sell as our leisure time and even our homes are viewed by some as primarily a commodity, another means to money, rather than fulfilling their role as shelter for us and our family.

The less we consider this bigger picture, the more we can be overcome by immediate concerns, rather than putting them in perspective. If we consider other people rather than just ourselves it can help to broaden our horizons. The tighter knit the community in which we live, the more we tend to help one another. Recognition of our neighbours is just one step towards seeing that there is more to life than just fulfilling our own needs. Yet getting to know those around us can seem like a major step and that is still a million miles away from considering the extent of the physical reality we occupy. 93 million miles from us is our sun. It provides heat and light for us all and yet how many times do we actually recognise the true miracle of its role in our lives? Another level away, removed even from our physical reality is the spiritual life and how many of us think about this or actually put effort into recognising this all-encompassing sphere? The more something is removed from the perception of our five senses, the less we are likely to include it in our perspective and yet we are living our spiritual lives right now.

Luckily, our emotions and our intuition are there to inform our perspective and in recognising the role that both play in our lives, we have another angle from which to view and address the world. Today, in a modern society we may rarely even sit under open sky or watch a sunset, let alone get involved in nature. Ancient civilisations such as the Inca, Aztec and the ancient Egyptians were so involved in the growth of their crops and the turning of the stars that the natural world was a huge part of their lives; in many ways it was their existence, integral to everything they did. They lived as part of the world, without separation and partly because of the immediacy of nature, they embraced their spirituality to help them better understand the meaning of life. Merely existing in nature, its harsher aspects and its beauty can be a journey of discovery for our soul.

Perversely, the development of technology has removed us from direct involvement with our environment. We are now less likely to have a daily relationship with the natural world, to benefit from the influence of the Earth and experience the wonders of natural growth. Instead of experiencing, we find the world through our televisions, computers or books. We forget our home is sitting on a globe, that our office building may be protruding into a vast sky or that while the images on our TV screens project images of foreign lands, we could just as easily have been born in those places, or that the people suffering wars and famine are actually our global neighbours.

So it is that we can live our lives in a way that only deals with the immediate, blinkered to all else, or we can go a step further and recognise the physical world around us and how interconnected it is, or we can take our evolution one step further still and consider our place as a spiritual being in a spiritual universe, learning and progressing our spiritual goals.

How do we grow with life?

We are at a stage where society has a pressing need to once more join in a common purpose and to develop a spiritual element within its priorities. Sadly, much of our purpose is currently expressed in very narrow ways, as individuals striving for personal and perhaps familial survival or taking forward the goals of our work lives. We have no great common goal and it can feel like we are struggling with one another to survive. We recognise base human motives in those around us and suspect and vilify our political leaders, our royalty and national identity is no longer a unifying element in our lives, while our religious framework and structure is fragmented by misunderstanding and lies.

If we reject social conscience, religious solidarity and leadership from anything other than our own opinions, what purpose is served by our lives? To live longer? To be fitter? To be healthier physically? Where is our growth? Where is the ultimate purpose?

In one sense, our soul is like a computer and what we put into it is what it can learn and grow with. There is no doubt that at the moment in many areas of society we are prioritising the wrong elements. Instead of focusing on life as a journey of growth, we are all hoping to find fulfilment and perhaps seeking it in our material growth or to wall off the woes of the world and ensure our own comfort. Society therefore has a big role to play in providing the backdrop to our aspirations. However, we have complete freedom of choice as to what we seek from life, what we prioritise and how we choose to approach it. Therefore, the responsibility and the rewards for how we live are ours alone.

Each physical life is like a train we board. The track is laid out and we have a ticket that begins at the station marked 'birth' and ends at the terminus of physical death. Within the train we are free to choose where we sit and what role we aspire to. We can be in the engine compartment working hard to ensure progress, a fulfilling but sometimes thankless task, in the driver's cabin taking control of our situation, where we shoulder responsibility and all the demands it brings, or sitting in the carriages and being carried throughout our lives. At every stage of our journey we have a choice as to whether we wish to take control. For the onus is on us to realise our passage has options. It is up to us whether we can find the way forward that empowers us, to find an outlet that feeds life. Or we can take the default position and languish in the mistaken belief that life is out of our control and therefore has little meaning for us. Happiness can be ours and it is up to us to choose to embrace the journey or not. For the role we play not only affects us, there are countless people of every sort for us to interact with and whose company we can enjoy. All are seeking happiness and all are on a spiritual journey.

There are many different types of experiences on our journey. Some of us are travelling through emotional wastelands, some are having an exciting time with many stops along the way and for some the journey feels mediocre and we wish the service we received was better! For others still, the journey is recognised as but one train ride on a vast network of potential destinations and experiences we will have over countless lives.

We each have a beginning point when we board the train, yet none of us know where our tracks end. Like Pandora's Box, once the door opens to our carriage, infinite possibilities present themselves and with our opportunity for travelling to our chosen destination comes the chance we may fail in our goals and fall short of our stop.

There are many types of journey we can embark upon. Some are on inner journeys of fulfilment. Others are on a journey to prove to themselves that they can fulfil physical goals, while others still may be here to experience human relationships in their myriad forms and learn through them. We may be here to bear responsibility and test ourselves as to whether we can handle it. Alternatively, our main purpose may be to help others and bring some good to the world, whether it be our family, friends or the whole of the human race.

Each of us can have a mission that suits our nature and our attributes. A person born to achieve a position of leadership and learn to live with it cannot spend a disproportionate amount of time helping the sick, nor can someone who is here to embody caring spend their time seeking a position of power if they are to find personal fulfilment. What is right for one person and not for another can be found within, through the sense of fulfilment we gain and this can guide us to recognise our purpose in life.

The vast majority of us do not know the ultimate purpose of our journey, how it might feel to take it or where it will end. It is good that we do not know because with no guarantee of success, with no awareness of spirit world, we experience the full commitment that life demands as we embark upon it and the joy of new experiences and surprise. We are not totally in the dark however, we are given everything we need to spur us on to full involvement. We all have things that fulfil us, be it a yearning to create through art, to learn and explain through science, to create order through the use of mathematics, to care and to heal, to serve and protect or to journey and learn by meeting those of every culture. Nurses, artists, doctors, engineers, politicians, prison officers, decorators, mechanics, policemen, firemen, teachers, lawyers, farmers, accountants and spiritual practitioners all have their place and each role that is available to us down here provides the potential for fulfilling the goals we are here to achieve. With such an abundance of potential roles, there are countless ways to fulfil our journey.

The time we spend on Earth may be long or short, but every life has a purpose and the potential for true meaning. It is what we take back with us at the end of our journey that matters most, and we have the pleasure of enjoying life, creating, loving, living in joy, expressing our passions and learning along the way.

What we choose, who we associate with and how fast we travel, will teach us what type of people we wish to be with and what example we wish to follow. A spiritual pathway helps us to identify with our inner-self, recognise that there is a bigger picture and provide options. In this way, we can gain the maximum enjoyment from life, not least because we are freer of regret and indecision.

By opening ourselves to life, we make room to enjoy and truly appreciate every element of the world in which we live. The gift of our body allows us to experience everything, an amazing vehicle that takes us where we want to go. Space, nature, all are incredible.

At the end of our journey, we can appreciate that the hardest times deliver the biggest rewards, because trials and tribulations are what deliver the greatest learning. By finding ourselves, we can understand how we react to life and what the best way forward is. Learning through life may seem hard at the time, but the discovery that comes with it can be incredible. Realisation is not about finding our shortcomings, it is about growth and growing through life demands that we get actively involved.

Chapter Nine - The Higher Self

We have already discussed the soul and how it relates to us. Yet, there is another aspect of our being that resides in the realm of the universal energy and seeks to act out, through our lives, the collective consciousness it holds. This collective consciousness is our True or Higher Self.

The Higher Self, while it is part of us and exists in spirit world is a separate entity to the soul. As the body serves a purpose as a vessel for the soul to enable it to progress, so the soul wishes to reach the level of its highest realisation, which is the Higher Self.

The Higher Self is a thought process that is there to guide us and connect the soul and us to God in a way that retains not only the soul's knowledge, but also the bigger plan for our existence. The soul is on a journey, while the Higher Self is a template that is connected to our soul, God and the Universe. In a sense, the Higher Self is the plan for us that maps out what we are and what we are to achieve. At the same time it is not the expression of that achievement, nor the realisation of it; rather like a mould, it sets out the shape we are here to fulfil. So while the soul is the repository of our experience and learns through life, the Higher Self retains the shape of what we are yet to become. As such, the Higher Self houses much knowledge of the plan for us. While the soul is an inner feeling that tells us whether what we are doing is right for this spiritual element of our lives, the Higher Self is like a neural network of knowledge that holds the ideal plan for our lives throughout the ages, alongside the blueprint of what we are when we are entirely whole.

When we pass over our soul brings back the learning of that most recent lifetime to our Higher Self, which absorbs that knowledge. Our Higher Self then retains and integrates all the information of all our lives and checks what it is we have learned against our overall mission. What we need next learn is then determined and the Higher Self instructs the soul as to our next learning imperative that will bring us closer to the fulfilment of our Higher Self's overall plan. So the Higher Self holds the questions that are yet to be answered through our existence and checks what we have learned against those questions. The more questions we answer physically through how we behave and learn in life, the closer we come to passing our overall exam. So, the combination of our soul, our Higher Self and our physical life is the totality of what we are. The Higher Self knows what we are to achieve, the soul feels the imperative of our mission and the physical body is the vehicle for each mission towards that goal.

The Higher Self is our own individual blueprint for our philosophy and the meaning of life for us. It is both the mission on which we are engaged and our higher consciousness.

We are a manifestation of the thought process held by our Higher Self as well as a vehicle for our soul's wish to develop and experience. The Higher Self could not exist without the soul and every soul has a Higher Self which God creates.

We already know that each Soul, once born into existence, wishes to learn through direct experience. It is this imperative which creates the need for a physical body, a vehicle through which each of us is fulfilling our soul's journey.

Only in the most extreme of self-inflicted circumstances can a body survive without a soul and that is when we have acted to diminish it, to the extent that our soul dies within us. When a person has become so out of control that they are governed solely by their physical needs and desires, when they have succumbed to the temptations that can corrupt us, then they are in conflict with both the needs of the Higher Self and the soul. When we engage in enough negativity and selfish behaviour, eventually we lose our selves. If we do it maliciously and for long enough we can diminish our soul, even to the extent that it leaves us or dies. The Higher Self and the soul can exist without the physical body, but if we act in extremely negative ways and our soul leaves us, we walk the Earth like an empty shell, devoid of conscience, empathy, love and all the spiritual attributes that are in accordance with the Higher Soul's plan and our soul's needs.

The Higher Self is the collective thought of ourselves, it is also the collective thought of God through which He knows each of us individually. The Higher Self is our highest manifestation, the reason and the conscience, the highest aspiration of what we can be, the fulfilment of what we are and the blueprint we were created to fulfil. The Higher Self is the connection between our soul and all the spiritual realms, while the soul connects our body with the Higher Self where all souls dwell in Spirit of World between lives.

The Higher Self is like a computer neural network that connects everything within us to everything without. The soul is like the hard drive which records everything we do and the body is the keyboard through which we enter our experiences. So as our soul and our body join together as one, the Higher Self is the balancing factor that reminds us of the overall plan, connects our soul with it and is the repository for the direction in which our personal course proceeds.

By acting in accord with the dual influences of our Higher Self and our soul, we are able to fulfil the ultimate purpose of our life on Earth.

The Higher Self as part of our journey
When a soul progresses to the highest stage it can accomplish and no longer has need of a physical body, we have achieved that part of the plan our Higher Self mapped out for our physical lives. The soul then embarks, in accordance with the blueprint of our Higher Self, on a journey to become complete in the world of spirit; to join fully with our Higher Self and to unite in full realisation of its goals.

This spiritual element of our journey may entail us in becoming Guides or Teachers in the world of spirit as we continue on our pathway of progression and to further our goal of becoming fully complete.

This overall journey of unification may take millennia to complete and when we have reached this ultimate goal in the world of spirit, our soul and Higher Self can manifest as a singular entity with a continuity of thought that allows us to realise ourselves as a discrete, complete individual. In other words, once we have progressed far enough in our spiritual journey we no longer have need of a physical body to represent our boundaries and we then achieve our perfect state of consciousness in the world of spirit. For us to reach this stage we must have achieved total perfection and the Higher Self exists as a reminder of what we are and what we are yet to become.

Connecting with your Higher Self

Connecting with our Higher Self is an ambitious goal we may strive for, but it is not a process we can control, rather it is a door we may open that then allows our Higher Self to join with us. So while we may have every need for it, we cannot force it to happen. Instead we must allow ourselves to let go to the extent that we are ready for it to come to us.

To be at this point, we must want to better ourselves and seek to be at one with ourselves in both a physical and spiritual sense. We must want to be connected to the very core of all of existence, to be at one with ourselves and with all of life.

The concept of our Higher Self is not some theoretical ideal, it is an energetic element of us that we can connect with to naturally progress our own spiritual evolution. Connecting to the Higher Self is a journey to meet with our ultimate state. If we achieve this link we are privileged, because we have attained a state of being where we are totally at one with ourselves in this lifetime. To allow our

Higher Self to connect we need to let go of all limiting emotions, so that we may let in that which is always with us.

Taking a spiritual perspective

Remembering that we are spiritual beings first and therefore, physical beings serving a spiritual purpose is the key to facing life's challenges. Knowing that there is a higher purpose helps us to look at things objectively, considering our role in life and the bigger picture of what we are here to achieve for our soul, for our Higher Self and our karma.

Without this realistic, flexible outlook, we can find ourselves viewing life's challenges as though we are a prisoner to our obstacles, not seeing the wood for the trees, trapped in our own viewpoint or lost in our own thoughts. A truly spiritual perspective gives us far greater freedom to address life step-by-step, separating out our feelings as well as we are able and recognising with greater clarity what best to do for ourselves and others. For much of the negativity we experience is our reaction to life and while this may be justifiable and understandable, the more we restrict ourselves by adhering to our narrow perspective, the more our frustrations, our sense of injustice and feelings of hurt can take control.

Typically, from time-to-time, life will present us with situations that swamp our emotions. We may become overwhelmed with grief, anxiety, anger, revenge, jealousy, loneliness and all manner of negativities. The more we comprehend the reasons, the root cause of these feelings, the more we can understand ourselves and deal with these limiting emotions in a way that enables us to move on.

Addressing ourselves is the way to create real and lasting change. If we recognise that there is a bigger plan that we are all part of and that we have complete free will in how we decide to act, it enables us to choose a direction that serves a positive purpose. A spiritual outlook offers us a means to comprehend the bigger picture, the means to determine why we feel bad when we encounter certain situations, the mental freedom to find a positive way forwards and the solid means to achieve it. This approach improves our ability to deal with life and achieve far greater peace of mind.

Spiritual leadership

Many people are looking for something more, a greater meaning and perhaps solace from the pain that is inherent in our physical and emotional lives. We seek something or somebody that transcends all else and brings us an answer, a route to love and all the good feelings of camaraderie and kinship that should be part of everyday life.

When we find someone or some message that brings this spiritual insight to our lives, we can identify so strongly with the spiritual figures that are sent to help us find the way, that we make Gods and idols of those who are, in essence, human like ourselves. Our tendency is to identify with those who educate us to the idea of something greater and wish them to be perfect, perhaps supernatural spiritual beings devoid of any fault or limiting human attribute.

These perfect beings do exist, in spirit world, but when any of us takes birth in human form, while we may have the most pure and divine nature and a spiritual destiny to fulfil, yet we are still human. We are all God's Children, perfect in our creation by Him and yet still on our journey of life. Therefore, we are right to aspire to spiritual progression and to revere those who give us hope of a life after death.

Yet we must remember that perfection resides in God. He is the source of everything we encounter in the physical world. For recognising His love brings us the opportunity for development and growth, without the threat of pain or loss. With it, we can both recognise the deeper needs within ourselves and learn how much of that which we suffer in the physical world is the result of our own behaviour. When we encounter those who are able to acquaint us with the wider spiritual universe and provide us with the means to recognise what lies within our own hearts, so we can find ourselves lodging all our hopes and wishes for happiness with these heralds. So strong is our wish to find something perfect that we may elevate those who bring a message, with which we can relate, to a position of unquestionable authority. Yet it is what we are able to find for ourselves and within ourselves that is the true message. What counts most is that which shines a light on ourselves and illuminates life's bigger picture.

The message Jesus brought was one of love, the Buddha called upon us to be a light unto ourselves and the great spiritual leaders are those that point the way to greater understanding and love. Part of what we see in them and their words is a way of being fully ourselves, unhindered by doubt, because we have found the answers. The tenets they introduce are advice on how each of us might live more fulfilling and happier lives and yet, because we see in their words a greater truth, the temptation is to impose this illumination as a set of rules on those around us, citing our spiritual leaders as authorities on how others might live their lives. Were we perfect, we would have no need of leadership and were life perfect, we would live in harmony with no need of guides. For the teachings of our Earthly spiritual guides are that much more powerful if we recognise that they are human beings like ourselves and it is their outlook and vision that elevates them to the position of authority we convey upon them.

Each and every one of us is human first and there are none amongst us who can escape physical reality. Therefore for our own peace of mind, we must recognise that our own emotions and attitudes are both a reflection of who we are, just as much as who we are is reflected in how we act. So, to become our own spiritual messenger, we must address our own selves and bring to light what it is that we find most meaningful in life. This does not mean embarking necessarily on a great spiritual journey, unless we wish to, because the most meaningful spiritual journey is merely that which naturally leads us to inner clarity and happiness. Once we have learned to communicate honestly within, we become not only a light unto ourselves, but, potentially, to those around us.

Beyond our inner journey in any given life there is a greater journey each of us are taking. By recognising ourselves spiritually, we grow. By embodying love and helping those around us, regardless of whether we view life as a spiritual journey or not, we find ourselves in a place called Heaven. By living a spiritual and loving life, we journey upwards within this realm, being recognised for who we are and increasing our ability to recognise the higher levels of Creation, because we have embodied the higher aspirations within ourselves. Our true destiny is to elevate ourselves spiritually and from the moment we take this pathway on Earth, we find it difficult to turn away from. For the spiritual pathway opens up a life of deeper meaning, inner fulfilment and allows us to gain increasing clarity as to what is worthwhile, while everything else is put into perspective.

So it is, by pursuing a spiritual journey here, gaining knowledge and experience, we progress on our journey in spirit world and can eventually reach a position where we might become fully embodied there. The next step in our evolution once we have reached this position, is to become a guide and then a teacher in the world of spirit, helping souls on Earth in their own development and progression. True spiritual leadership is found within and it naturally grows the more we encourage it inside ourselves. So, spiritual leaders are made, just as much as they are born.

Chapter Ten - Spirit World

For us here on Earth, there are many ways of finding and identifying with the spiritual universe. There are methods that open us to our own energy, help us connect with spirit world, join with the universal energy and find God. There are many routes to incorporating each of these into our lives.

If we choose a religious pathway, then we can take the tenets of that religion, its spiritual leaders, its customs and observances as our guides. Alternatively we can open ourselves to spiritual thought of all denominations and widen our minds so that we realise our own beliefs. Another option is to develop our intuitive senses or clear vision or clairvoyance. This particular pathway can enable us to gain our own insight into the nature of the spiritual universe and, importantly, ourselves.

If we develop clairvoyance or clear vision, we can learn to explore the immense, magnificent spiritual levels that are open to us, connect with those who dwell there and journey through this vast universe of energy that emanates from God. For He is the ultimate source of our souls and we are part of His spiritual world, which is populated in energy-form by every living thing. If we are able to find these areas for ourselves and connect with them, it can help us gain a clearer perspective on, not only the role of our human life but of our spiritual journey here on this Earth and in spirit world.

We do not necessarily need to know the whole picture at the outset, but finding just one piece of evidence that the spiritual universe exists, one irrefutable fact we can relate to for ourselves, opens the doorway to a vast universe of learning.

In His Image
Here on Earth, we are contained in bodies that live encompassed by a physical world that lies outside of us and with which we connect

through our senses. God, by contrast, is the centre of all things, yet encompasses them. What He has created lies within His domain, within His consciousness.

Human beings are made in His image, yet on a vastly smaller scale. We live within reality, whereas God, by contrast, is all of reality. Therefore there is nothing in our reality that is outside of Him and, all His world is contained within Him. The universal energy which emits from Him is a natural consequence of His existence. Each of us in the physical universe exists like cells within His body and each of us has our own independent existence, but are part of His greater form. He contains everything, while reality exists outside of us and we therefore live in His world. We are said to be made in His image because like Him, within each of us dwells our own reality of cells, all of which lies within our consciousness.

Spirit world

Spirit world is the name we give to that wider area of spiritual energy that encompasses the denser physical reality we inhabit. So while our physical reality may seem separate from the world of spirit, we also lie within it and are able to access it through our psychic senses. Both spirit world and physical reality are equally part of Creation.

God's wish to grow lead Him to create a wider manifestation of Himself. To do this, he created souls and these entities in turn needed a place to inhabit. Inevitably, God created a physical reality for His children, at once meeting our needs and His own.

Each of our souls has made the choice to manifest through physical bodies, so that we too might grow and come to a greater state of realisation.

This is why we are able to say 'as above so below' because we are living out in a microcosm, the same process God has chosen for Himself. Like Him, we are made up of an entire universe of cells that are both manifestations of our choice to grow and necessary for us to connect with life. We are physical microcosms of His all-embracing macrocosm which encompasses both physical and spiritual reality.

Below God, in spirit world, we find everything that is and everything that is yet to be. There are 12 levels or spheres in spirit world, the 'lowest' or 'first' seven of these realms occupied by our human souls.

Level one is inhabited exclusively by those souls who are no longer permitted a human birth. Higher up, levels two to six are where our human souls dwell both during and in-between physical incarnations, while level seven is reached only by those spiritually progressed souls who no longer require human incarnation to experience and learn what life has to offer.

It can, however, be misleading to think of these levels as segregated floors, rather we can think of them as spheres or bands of spiritual existence.

Visualise a rainbow and the seven different layers of colour within it and this is one way of understanding how the levels of human spiritual existence lie side by side. Now imagine that each of the colours represents a level or sphere in spirit world. In each level, we find souls all of whom are developing so that they might progress higher. Each level has numerous areas of existence within it and each area has a focus of development and learning. For the inhabitants of each level are on a journey of spiritual progression and will need to study in much the same way we do if we wish to progress in our physical existence. Those who seek beauty will learn an appreciation of music or art and those who wish to appreciate their fellow souls will seek out areas in which to socialise and interact. However, it is only here on Earth that we can fully test and apply the skills we are keen to develop in the world of spirit.

Wherever we are in spirit world, we are constantly seeking to expand and grow, to elevate ourselves to a better position where we can exist amongst those who have already attained a higher place. Our souls can work very hard to achieve these ends. Yet, it is when we return to Earth in a physical body that we may be truly tested and the way in which we react will determine our next direction.

The lowest or first level in spirit world is occupied by those that have passed beyond redemption. These are the very worst souls that have repeatedly worked negatively in life after life, developing no redeeming features and eradicating all glimmer of humanity. This level is a living nightmare, where each soul recalls and relives, time and time again, all the bad deeds they have committed in life. On this level, each and every contact with another soul reignites a memory of some negative act, when they chose to harm rather than heal a situation or person in their physical lives. Here, we find those souls that have ignored all their chances, held malicious intentions and acted upon them. They will have deliberately embraced cruelty, chosen a path of violence and destruction and done so time and time again in one life after another, until they have eradicated all that is good within them and become truly evil.

These souls are those in need of the greatest healing. Yet, sadly at this level, this healing cannot come and their only option is for them to be restricted from further physical lives, not as a punishment, but rather because they have exhausted all the opportunities to elevate themselves from the mire of their own making. All redeeming qualities have been lost and these souls are banished upon returning to spirit world, the last vestiges of their identity taken from them and their energy sent out into oblivion, so that they are truly and finally lost to themselves.

While this distinct minority of souls have deprived themselves of their own humanity, there is a tiny glimmer of hope if prayers are sent out for them. If these prayers are heard, then they are returned to level two, where they can be stripped of their old ways and cleansed, 'recycled' so that they might start on their journey once more.

On level two we find those souls who have amassed many negative and cruel acts over a number of lives, ignoring the chances they have been given, but where hope for redemption still remains because they have acted, in some way or other, selflessly to help others. For, if a shred of goodness remains within us, we always have the hope of rising higher. Souls on level two have the chance for another human life, the chance to prove themselves and rise up from where they are firmly lodged.

On level two, souls have a very limited recognition of one another and are wrapped up in a solitary and joyless, lonely existence. Imagine the absence of hope that constant selfishness will bring you when it is coupled with many negative acts. Thinking only of ourselves cuts us off from others and limits our ability to interact, both here and in spirit world. However, those without any hope would not rise to level two. Instead, those we find here have a vestige of hope, thanks to some positive acts they have performed during their lives. Here, they will have windows of opportunity to start again and make things right for themselves. If they fail to act upon these opportunities, they are taken off by the energy of spirit world to be recycled.

This recycling means that the soul is whisked away and their potential for harm removed. Any soul that is recycled will have the weight of its identity taken from it and be given the chance to start afresh. Like a hard drive that is wiped by a powerful magnet, these souls are spiritually cleansed so that all that remains is the soul, but with none of its memories, none of the weight of the past and none of the knowledge of that which came before. In a sense, they have themselves taken away from themselves and all that remains is the opportunity for the spark of life to renew itself.

Above the lower levels in spirit world are levels occupied by those souls that have progressed sufficiently to recognise themselves. Here are souls that have identified with their own conscience and therefore their responsibility to be accountable for their actions. On these middle levels we find all those of us who have lived a mixture of positive and negative lives. There are those who have loved and cared for each other, yet remain stubborn, those who have ignored the plight of others and yet done immense good for their family and friends and those who have lived lives that are neutral, neither giving out nor taking from those around them. This is where many of us dwell between lives on Earth.

So, on level three we find souls with humanity and only some conscience. This is not a place where a soul feels comfortable. For a soul to be in this area, it will have lead a limited physical life, focusing on its own selfish needs or being vindictive and greedy enough to harm other people. Upon passing over, the soul will experience the same limitations, living in an environment that reflects to it all that that has been given out in life. If we have lived and acted cruelly, our soul goes to an area where cruelty is the norm, because it has not identified with anything greater, nor does it deserve a higher position within spirit world. These souls will need to return to physical life, to redress their karma, to perhaps experience the same cruelty or selfishness they have put out in previous lives so that they might learn their lessons. However, if there is great enough remorse, then only the potential will be around them in their next physical life. Either way, the souls that fall within this category will be given the opportunity to embody the opposite to that which they have been. Therefore they will gravitate towards choosing lives which demand love, forgiveness and patience. Upon being born to Earth, each of these souls will have an inner feeling or knowing that acting without consideration for others is inherently wrong. This will be experienced as a feeling deep within, a conscience that they may act upon or ignore.

So, every action we take here has a very real and definite impact on not only this life, but also upon our immortal soul. Those that return to Earth and redress the balance are elevated within spirit world, while those that totally eradicate all tendencies towards a lack of kindness will have made further progress.

The lower levels need not concern us overly, but their presence serves to illustrate just how impactful it can be if we choose to fall prey to our own most negative impulses. For God does not dictate where our souls dwell, rather we build our own palaces and dig our own dungeons. If we believe this is the case, then we can recognise that this life is the most important opportunity we can possibly have to have a positive effect on each other and ourselves.

It is very important to know that having a hard life emotionally or physically does not indicate necessarily that we are a soul emerging from a lower level. We may have elevated ourselves to a higher position but have chosen this particular life as an opportunity to embody that which we aspire to. So a soul that has progressed positively over very many lifetimes may have a very tough life because it is perfecting its understanding and chose this incarnation to get over some of the final karmic hurdles that are on its pathway. Whatever life we are in is a very real opportunity to progress spiritually, to make the most of what we have and to do unto others that which we would have done unto ourselves.

Before we address level four it is very important to bear in mind that while we are describing levels, these spheres are all part of the same creation. There is no prescribed hierarchy and yet we created one by our choice of learning through a physical life. For in spirit world we gravitate as high as we wish to, as we learn the lessons that enable us to do so. In the same way that we can only become an artist with materials such as paint, pencil, stone or ink, so to realise ourselves fully in spirit world we must experience the good or the bad in each physical life, learning as we do so, what feelings sit most comfortably with us. For all of us are prey to negative thoughts or may be overcome by emotions, but it is what we choose to act upon that is important to us spiritually. Someone who has the toughest life, yet maintains a positive attitude and helps others has maintained their inner-self. If they have realised forbearance and patience when they might easily have reacted negatively, they have become all the more 'real' and they have learned a very valuable lesson to take back to their soul. Wholesomeness is a result of being true to ourselves and considering others, no matter what the adversity and, so it is that a tough life can be our soul's salvation. Here on Earth this can seem like the most unfair and unreasonable part of life, for how often do we see people in dire circumstances who still manage to make the best of it? However much we might rebel against the way in which life challenges us, or treats those around us, so it is necessary to recognise the way in which we can work with these circumstances. Lessons may be learnt through hardship and appreciation may come from deprivation. Beauty can be revealed to us in our ability to recognise what is truly meaningful. Friendship and light heartedness are often found amongst those who have very little else and yet, that is when we know the bonding is true and the camaraderie is real, for it seeks nothing more than the wellbeing of community.

It is this sense of caring and recognition of others that is found on level four. Here we can find those souls that are crossing the boundary into a spiritual recognition of themselves and of life. These souls will have a perception of the preciousness of life. The souls on level four are not fully spiritually realised and yet they are gravitating to level five. If we look at the inhabitants of levels four and five, where most of our souls dwell, this feels like a nice level of existence, where we find decent, everyday folk. There is no negative miasma as one might find on level two, so the inhabitants are not wrapped up in their misery and woe and therefore have a feeling of much greater clarity. There will be very many positive reasons or ways in which a soul may achieve these levels, spheres or states of being.

At every level, there are very many areas, occupied by all types of souls. Just as we have personalities here and we all differ in our make-up, so there are very many different soul colourations.

On levels four and five we will find souls who arrive after countless lives of endeavour, with much hard work and learning behind them, those that have often made the choice to act positively when faced with a negative situation, and those that have chosen to care for others at personal cost. Whatever the impetus that has driven these souls higher, they all share a common heritage of having acted out of the very best of intentions.

Level five is a boundary between those who are still looking to material life to fulfil them and those that are finding themselves through human relationships and developing a less worldly view of the circumstances that confront them in life. Here we find those that are on the cusp of progressing into a realised spiritual journey for their soul.

On level six we find those souls that are really making progress. They have given up on many of the negativities that plague us and may have been through many lives to reach this level, or perhaps learned their lessons early. Here we find those who, though they still have much to learn, have overcome many of their inner challenges. Their next lives on Earth would be there to take them further in this journey and, unless they take a backwards step, their inner compass is pointing them higher in spirit world. They might, in the next physical life find themselves amongst a loving family, in circumstances that enable them to spread the love they have within them, or seeking a relationship which will take them forwards positively. Here on Earth we will recognise them for their inner wisdom, caring nature, or their natural ability to give good advice. We may see them as naturally loving and patient. They might be found in professions where they teach or care for those around them, or be recognised amongst their family as being a special person who is both good mannered and gentle. They might also have within them the spark of creativity which is the reflection of the depth of knowledge they possess within. A soul that is on this level would seek bonding within life, through family and friends, building a stable community around them. Typically they will have a positive effect, having an affinity for nature and perhaps animals, and always leaving a positive legacy for those who come to know them.

On level seven, we find a true spiritual level. Those souls who have completed their curriculum of learning will reside here. They have no more need to come down to Earth and gain further knowledge through a physical body. However, because of their level of progression they may wish to reincarnate to have a positive effect on life. Their motivation for coming back to Earthly life would be entirely positive and good, perhaps to be an artist who will bring beauty, a politician who would want to elevate people from poverty, a spiritual leader to bring love, an engineer who can bring communities together by building physical bridges or a journalist wishing to bring truth to our media. Wherever there is an opportunity to bring peace, community, love, bonding and beauty, so a soul on level seven might wish to come and live through yet another life that serves a positive purpose. That life may not be easy, nor pleasant necessarily, but the motivation for that soul would be to have a positive impact on the world.

Once we reach level seven, we may not wish to return to the Earth. Instead we have the choice to take up a role in spirit world. In our soul forms, we will here have reached a very high level of consciousness and there will be many ways in which we could help those who are on every level, whether it be through a physical rebirth or embodying in spirit world our wish to help others. For instance, we could play a role as a teacher for the young souls, passing on our experience of worldly things, making them aware of what to expect and easing their journey as much as we might, so that they are best prepared for what is to come in their next life. The higher we progress, the more choices we have, the more beautiful the surroundings on that level and the more blissful and harmonious the feelings we encounter. On level seven there are a plethora of beautiful sights, sounds, smells and feelings. There we will find academies of music and prayer, vast beautiful fields and forests, with animals and insects living in tranquillity. Everything we find there belongs, has its place and serves a purpose as part of the common unity. On this level in particular, our soul is that much more aware of the presence of God and the higher levels, it is heightened because the purpose of those who dwell here is to serve the Higher purpose. That is not to say we progress to this level that we might begin to serve His purpose, but that those who dwell here, do so because they have already lived lives that have naturally served that purpose. Therefore it matters not whether we were believers or followers of any given religion during life, but rather we recognised that there was a greater purpose to be served by life itself. Those who have an understanding and recognition of human life, will dwell here. They will have a deep understanding that humanity continues on its journey and would work to serve this end. Those who are here are patient, giving, kind and grateful and all of these attributes stem from their ability to embody love. So here we will find those who have been through many lives, learning their lessons to the full and appreciating that they are better for having learned them. This means that they will have lived, loved, appreciated the good and the bad and developed humility and the ability to truly care for those around them. Having become beautiful they live in the most beautiful of surroundings.

The position we hold in spirit world is the result of our life lived here. Yet, there, in our energy-form, we are most truly what we are. There is no disguising ourselves and our true light shines forth. So envy, jealousy and self-doubt are not felt there. These feelings are exclusively felt on Earth. Yet, if we find ourselves on a lower level, we might feel the shame of some past actions and wish to improve. Similarly, if we are on a higher level, we might wish to expand our knowledge and broaden our horizons.

Making our own Heaven

When we pass over to spirit world, if we have lived a normal or a good life, we will be able to manifest all the things we wish for. However, the whole basis of spirit world is love and if we build an environment there that serves ourselves alone, it will be empty and lack meaning, eventually leaving us isolated and lonely. We can create any environment we wish, but if we create out of self-indulgence, it will be for all the wrong reasons and will not provide fulfilment. If we pass over and build ourselves a bar to drink alcohol in, we will soon tire of the empty soulless feelings that come with it. Anything built out of desire alone, whether it be in spirit world or here on Earth, is a bottomless pit that will never give us what we are looking for.

If, instead, we chose to build because we have the needs of others in mind, or wish to create and share, we are joining with the purpose of life and opening to the reason spirit world exists to further ourselves and to live in harmony. In spirit world, we build best when we build as an expression of our love for others, or even for the love of the good things in life. So we may create gardens to share, playgrounds for children to play in, beautiful pictures, or homes for our loved ones. All these things are possible if they are done for the right reasons. For the foundation of everything that aids our progression in spirit world is love.

The more aware and complete we are in our thoughts, the more refined our consciousness, the higher we have progressed and the more conscious we are when we pass over. A highly advanced person who passes over will be able to bring into being all that they wish for and is only limited to what they deserve and what they have earned. Good people are able to create because they have earned the right and they earn this right because they have lived with love in their hearts. So, a good conscience brings us a better consciousness, both here and in the spiritual realms.

True creation is an act of love and spirit world has innumerable houses and buildings built by those with a good heart. Husbands and wives make their own little places in heaven that are a reflection of what they would wish for their partners. Homemakers build homes, priests may build churches, those who love nature build gardens and landscapes and forests, those who love the sea can create their own beautiful shore lines and those who love music may join with others of like minds to perform.

Whenever a soul passes over, they are naturally drawn to like minds on the other side. This means we might be drawn to our family or to an area where fellow artists, musicians, doctors or healers naturally congregate. We might seek out architects or those who love outdoor games and sports; anything into which we enjoy putting our heart and soul will have an area where we can find like-minded souls.

Self-serving activities do not serve us well in spirit world. Activities that build the spirit and work with energy on Earth, such as classical martial arts continue to serve a purpose while body building and shooting guns have no place, for they relate to the physical alone. However, the pursuit of learning, of mathematics and justice perpetuate, for they further the mind and the spirit. There, we have no need to buy, sell, eat or consume, but what fulfils us is of paramount importance. The higher you go, the more you will find groups engaged in all manner of activities that serve the purpose of the common good. There, we create and learn all those skills that build our understanding, our spirituality and our ability to love and care for one another. So, building a house, plank by plank and brick by brick, sculpting and painting endure, for they are a demonstration of our love, helping us to express ourselves and our wish to give.

We can also find in spirit world, exactly what we have missed in life. Perhaps, if we have lived busy, crowded, stressful lives we may seek out our own mountain top to dwell in solitude for a while or if we crave interaction and company, we may find places to socialise and converse through our thoughts.

Conversation in spirit world is strange to our experience here on Earth. Here, we can quite easily hold a conversation with no experience of what the other person is talking to us about. Language is the medium through which we convey concepts, describe states of mind and objects. We can therefore understand something such as childbirth intellectually, even if we have not experienced it, relate to extreme emotional states and comprehend the height of a mountain, even if we have never been to one, because language is our intermediary.

In spirit world, we embody what we have experienced, therefore our soul can only truly communicate that which it has lived through and is encompassed by that which it is.

A soul can appreciate and seek to learn in spirit world, but what it picks up will be quite academic until it has experienced it fully in a physical life. Therefore, if we have never eaten a cake in life, we cannot comprehend or identify the taste or smell of a cake in spirit world and if we try to create a cake without having made or tasted one in life, it would be a poor facsimile of the true experience. If a soul has never experienced child birth, it cannot relate to it. This is one reason why physical life is so important; it helps us to build our library of experience and relate to each other through shared understanding.

So, if our soul's main concern is to help those who have had emotional problems, it will need to have experience of those same problems. If our soul wants to relate to gardening, it will need to experience the joy of working with the soil and plant-life on Earth.

Activities that are spiritual in nature such as healing and prayer are things we can appreciate fully in spirit world. There, however, they cannot be tested through the adversity of life, which is what makes them a challenge here on Earth. Our aspirations can be honed in spirit world, but it is embodying them that creates experience and builds our characters and true learning comes from doing. So, even though spirit world gives us an environment saturated with divine love, where we are safe and secure with no threats, in a sense we are restricted there, because we cannot fully engage in all the activities we find in physical life. However, this is not felt as a restriction, it is merely a reflection of the fact that spirit world serves our soul and it has no need for buying, selling, consuming or persuading one another. Instead, there we exist in the full completeness of that which we are.

In spirit world, we can find all levels of experience and younger souls can be innocent of knowing all the pain that comes with Earthly life and can crave the experience of living on Earth. However, souls that have had an experience of the pain that comes with life might think twice before returning. While spirit world gives us all the inner feelings we need, this Earthly world has the potential to give us all we feel we need and the experience we desire compels us to seek out physical life.

So it is that if we have learnt everything we need to be whole we stay up in spirit world, and if we feel we need to learn more, we return to physical life. Yet if we wish to give, we can come down to help others as an expression of our compassion. There are other souls still, those who are more advanced, who seek to serve a higher purpose and better themselves. They can seek out life, even though their journey on Earth is complete, so that they might enhance their understanding, learn more, complete their journey and ascend higher still.

There are no half-measures in spirit world. There our cup overflows with all the good things we have brought to ourselves by giving those same things to others. So if we have been true to ourselves and cared for others, we can understand the value of love. Then we can go to a place where love infuses every element of our existence and we are honest and complete. If we have been selfless and truly put others first, we will in all likelihood be loved by those on Earth and those feelings reach us in our heavenly existence. This is why it is so important to gain an appreciation of what is truly important in life, because our spiritual being is the fullest expression of who we are. The truly important elements of our nature and our experience are those that go with us when we pass to the other side. Whatever good we do in life comes back to us two fold. We gain an appreciation of ourselves if we act on our better nature and we have the rewards of knowing that we have given of our best. We also enhance our existence in our energy-forms and create all the beautiful things that we have found on Earth, in Heaven. There, our love will be our sustenance, our compassion brings us companionship, our inner nature draws us to like-minded people and we create an inner landscape that is mirrored for us in Heaven's beautiful vistas.

Many of us here struggle and strive to make a life that gives us what we want, but whether we are successful or not, what we truly need can come from this struggle, whether it is inner-strength, patience, or a better understanding of the purpose that life serves.

It is not that which confronts us that is important, as much as what we learn from it. Therefore, a worker in the fields can take as much from life as a politician, all that separates each of us is the intentions and motivations we choose to follow. If we take love as our guide and appreciate that all of us are in the same boat, even recognising those who have fallen overboard and how they too are struggling, we are on the right course.

Perhaps the most important thing we can find out for ourselves about spirit world is the truth of our existence. The ramifications of knowing there is a place our soul returns to and that all the most fulfilling feelings exist there, is almost enough in itself. Yet if we journey further and find out about spirit world, it can provide us with a far wider perspective, not just on the potential of our spiritual journey, but on the wonderful emotional landscapes that can open for us if we choose to treat our physical journey as one that fulfils our spiritual goals.

So, when we find the gardens, the colours and wonderful scenery up there, we can appreciate just how important it is to be able to commune with nature here. Being able to appreciate the inner-fulfilment we get when we lose ourselves in beautiful scenery here, even for just a few brief moments, gives us a clue as to what it feels like for our soul to dwell in such an environment for eternity.

Spirit world is the bigger picture that we are all part of, and knowing that it is there can put physical life in perspective. For, whatever we do in life that is positive will aid us on the other side. For instance, when we find camaraderie on Earth with like-minded people, it is a signpost that we are developing the kind of warm-hearted openness that will attract like-minded souls on the other side; while acting as carer or provider for those who are sick or weak shows us the potential for inner fulfilment when we labour for the sake of others. This is also the preserve of the higher levels, the teachers and guides in spirit world.

For those who have a particularly tough existence, knowing there is a spiritual realm can offer hope. It shows us that life does have a purpose and that there are many souls who do care. For those who labour without seeming reward, we can find reassurance that there is a purpose to everything we do and that inner rewards are just as valid, even if they are recognised by few. Spirit world is proof that our inner-self is more important than many of us suspect, for it continues beyond this one life.

We live in a physical reality and it can be difficult to comprehend how there can be an entirely different world with its own structure, architecture and laws that we cannot apprehend with our five senses. This is the key point that makes many of us question or disbelieve the spiritual element of life and the existence of a spiritual realm. If we cannot touch it physically, nor see it with our eyes, how can we say this place exists?

To perceive spirit world, we use senses other than the five we currently rely on here. It is another dimension linked with our own and in fact, could be said to have more reality than our physical existence. For our souls can exist without a physical existence, but we could not exist without our souls.

Embracing life

The physical world is here to enable us to realise our spiritual purpose and the spiritual world encompasses the Earth. This is yet another way of saying that our spiritual existence is of more importance than our Earthly one. However, our two existences, the spiritual and the Earthly are not exclusive, instead they are a union. Therefore the way we conduct ourselves here is of paramount importance to our soul. However, our two existences, the spiritual and the Earthly are not exclusive, instead they are a union and the way we conduct ourselves here is of paramount importance to our soul and to grow in the classroom of life.

What we do is an expression of who we are as much as it is a way of being a better person, which is the hidden goal of all our existences. When we take our journey from spirit world and come into each physical life, each time we are acting out the wishes of our soul. Our soul wants to progress and to grow and the classroom of life is where it can best realise this ambition. Yet, when life is full of despair, it can still cause us to question the point and purpose of it all.

Consciously or subconsciously, each of us develops an outlook in reaction to the challenges that face us. We are here to learn and the world, at this moment, is testing the majority of us in what sometimes feel like a harsh manner. Life challenges us, but conversely we can look to it to find our answers. It is life that helps us to find our limits and invites us to remain true to ourselves while we overcome the obstacles we face. Yet, it is life's lessons that educate us to what we find most fulfilling and its positives and negatives therefore go hand in hand.

While spirit world is a place of perfection, the physical world cannot be, for here we find ourselves dealing with imperfect situations and people. Physical life serves its spiritual purpose when we learn positive ways of dealing with it. For, once we have learned our lessons, we can move on and patience is its own reward, as is giving, loving and having the courage to care for those around us. Nothing lasts forever, yet our lives won't change until we have faced our insecurities and fears. So, by developing a greater understanding of people and of ourselves, we can find a better route for our own progression.

One of the best approaches we can take is to embrace life and appreciate what it offers, including its highs and lows and enjoy the mere fact that we are alive. To choose to better ourselves is one of the very best decisions we can make, because the best people are those who make an effort to understand, value what life offers and take time to care. If we are taking this approach, then we can rightly be proud of who we are.

However, pride is a loaded word. Pride can give us the false sense that we are better than those around us and can tempt us into judging those who do not share what we see as our positive attributes, or even our beliefs. Pride can be an unjustified self-regard that indicates we have an overinflated ego. By contrast, if we recognise our own positive attributes and also have a good measure of self-awareness, it can be a beneficial force in our lives as it imparts the confidence to pursue our goals.

If we are happy that we have done our best, then we can be proud of our efforts and happy with ourselves. This is a natural and very positive place to be. So we should always give ourselves recognition for making positive choices, for this acknowledgement can spur us on to greater efforts while enjoying the feeling that comes with doing something good for ourselves and others. There are many things we can feel proud about, yet in relation to the immensity of creation we are but one short lived grain of sand and recognising this can help us not be tempted into too high an opinion of ourselves.

Giving is a positive trait. Yet we should be honest with ourselves as to whether we are giving spontaneously and freely, or giving for what we hope we might receive in return. If we approach all life with self-honesty, we are far more likely to be successful at finding lasting happiness within. Self-honesty helps us to be self-aware and it means our choices are far more beneficial to us as a person.

Self-honesty also helps us through our tough times. If we are troubled and we are honest about it, then it gives us the chance to investigate why. Without focussing on the troubling feelings we can recognise them, be honest about their cause and focus on what we can do to move on. Whereas if we are not able to be honest with ourselves, our insecurities and inner issues hold sway. Sadly this can lead us to project our negativities onto the world and onto others and we become a source of potential trouble. If we are insecure, we can try to reassure ourselves by seeking power over others, when we should be seeking to gain power and control over ourselves instead. If we are full of woe and asking others to feel sorry for us, we can instead try and share our experience openly without seeking sympathy. If we are trying to make someone feel bad, why not choose to speak with honesty about how we feel, or what it is we are really seeking to impart. If this option is not open to us, we can always choose to hold our peace instead of adding to the world's woes and the unhappiness of others. Life is not static and if we are feeling uncomfortable, the more we work positively with it, the more freedom we will experience within our situation and ourselves until the time is ready for either to change.

For, the place for our control to manifest is in our self-control and the more we are aware of ourselves, the more clarity we have in our thoughts, adding power to our actions. Physical life gives rise to so many emotions and these show why we choose to come down here to live, for by testing ourselves with lives full of grit, we grow pearls of wisdom.

Growth is not our sole purpose for existing. Life is a rich soup for us to savour and merely by living it in harmony we can have the most beautiful of existences. Yet, it can be hard and we have all seen what happens when one person turns sour. Negativity can destroy the atmosphere in a room or trigger the negativities of those around us.

In physical reality, we create and live-out the results of our actions and this, in turn, creates who we are. In spirit world, it is our soul that is our vehicle, not the body. So, on Earth we can act a role, we can put forward what we want others to believe and people believe what they see of us. In spirit world, we are merely what we are and there is no other side to us. Therefore, the principle of being true to yourself reaps rewards throughout our entire existence. For, when we pass over, what we are is laid bare and we cannot hide our inner-self, run away, bluff or conceal the truth.

After death, our soul naturally gravitates to the sphere to which it is most suited and in which it has earned a place. Once we are between lives, we do not have the opportunity to create our karma. For there we are purely consciousness. So, while we may be on a high place in spirit world, there we do not have the opportunity to elevate ourselves further, until we are on the very highest levels. There, we are what we have already become. Here, we are creating what we will become.

Therefore karma is the natural mechanism that enables us to progress spiritually and the more we work with a positive motivation and for the right reasons, the more positivity will come back to us.

Chapter Eleven - The Geography of Spirit World

Spirit world exists to accommodate our souls and as such, serves as a manifestation of our needs for progression. On Earth, we were once greatly separated from one another by physical distance and natural barriers that kept us in distinct tribal groups. Gradually, over time, as migration and technological innovations have increased our ability to communicate across boundaries, these physical barriers have become less important.

Originally, each culture had characteristics that were strongly pronounced. Many of these still remain, but our knowledge of one another has increased and as residents of Earth we are, in many ways, less divided. Now, an African tribesman may well support the same football team as an Icelandic fisherman and a Chinese factory worker may aspire to embrace Western culture, while producing trainers that will be worn by a child in New York. While in the beginning we were exclusively divided by our dialects and our horizons were that much nearer, now we all have an opportunity to recognise ourselves as part of a global community of humanity.

In spirit world, when God first birthed our souls, we were all one. The original souls were few, only five existed and later, as we multiplied on Earth, God gave birth to an increasing number. Each soul then followed the karmic journey that was at once laid out for it and that it wished to follow. Our free-will took us in innumerable directions. Removed from our existence as energy, we each of us embarked on fantastic voyages of experience. We loved, lost and lived. We formed family-ties and worked together to survive. We touched the solidity of Earth and marvelled at a physical creation so splendid, that we could barely comprehend its endless diversity. So our reactions began. We held dear to those that we loved, both young and old. We cared for each other in caves, built walls to hold away danger and became angry with that which threatened our happiness. We cried at the loss of our nearest and dearest and learnt to survive through our physical pain. So, the physical closeness and the barriers between us were breeding grounds for our emotions and each area we occupied ensured a different type of national temperament, a distinct set of challenges and opportunities for growth. So, each soul would have many different types of environment, each with a leaning towards distinct types of experience and the way in which God had laid out our physical geography allowed us to grow and expand. For each of our souls craved this experience of life and all that it offers. Having taken our chances, life has now progressed from pre-history, through the many ages up to what is now the age of information. Yet, while the technology of our world has progressed and the barriers to communication have lessened, our ignorance means we still find reasons to fight viciously over our territorial and ideological differences.

In spirit world, there is no colour or status to divide our souls. We are all of us equal in God's eyes. However, where once no boundaries existed, we have expanded to populate vast areas and gradually each one has divided to allow for the sheer scope of experience, to accommodate our diverse interests, levels of growth, our wish for development and to provide fertile space for our souls to expand.

In spirit world our souls are born and each has ideas for experience. Some of these ideas are born with the soul, while others are the outcome of previous lives. Perhaps we have lived through a time of war and our main thought is to seek out experiences of healing and peace. Then our idea would launch our soul into a situation where we might be a nurse or doctor, a healer or a counsellor. Some souls are born from God specifically to fulfil a need for concepts to be brought to Earth. The idea of saving the planet, of engineering, creative expression and the development of medicine all come from concepts that are intellectual in nature, but many of the women and men who bring them here have an inner-drive to pursue their ideas. This inner-drive need not necessarily be pre-determined, it can be a direction we choose once we are born here, but for many, this inner drive is an expression of what they are born here to do. Tomorrow's chefs and engineers may be playing with toy kettles and screwdrivers from an early age, while our mathematicians are born with a natural flare and interest in numbers. Our artists appreciate the colours of nature and the sensory delights around them, while our gardeners have a love of the natural world. The families who farm provide experience for those who wish to live on the land, while those who fly the nest and seek out new experiences away from their families are today's explorers and hedonists. Sometimes, certain lives or elements of them are pre-ordained so that we might experience an aspect of existence, or fulfil a need, but come what may we are always able to make our own decisions and choose our own pathway, for all of life is an opportunity for our progression.

Therefore, the link between the geography of spirit world and that of Earth has a natural relationship and each is a reflection of the other. The connection between the two is maintained by our constant journeying between them. Our innermost needs are reflected in the geography of spirit world. The order and placement of each sphere enables us to naturally occupy the space we have earned, while the areas of interest we wish to pursue are catered for in halls of learning, libraries of information, halls for science, math, literature and museums. We can pursue our leisure in vast parks, boating lakes and auditoriums, while our spiritual needs are furthered in spirit world by witnessing God who is always above us and by connecting with like-minded souls. In spirit world, we can also pursue our spiritual goals by working in hospitals. These are areas prepared for those souls that are worn down when they pass over, so that they might convalesce and recuperate. There, we can exercise and become familiar with the pleasure of helping and giving as we familiarise ourselves with the myriad manifestations of emotional damage and spiritual shock physical life can inflict. So, the hospitals in spirit world are supremely important. For some souls pass unexpectedly and finding themselves without a body is a huge shock, while for those who have come across expecting oblivion, there is shock of a different nature. In both cases, our soul must once more become familiar with existing, yet being separate from the five senses, finding a place in Heaven and experiencing it as a level of consciousness not unlike a dream, but within a realm that has both form and natural laws, all of which exist outside of our consciousness and where we can create structures and fulfil our wishes according to our will, but without imposing that will upon others.

In spirit world, there are gathering places where we collect to pray for the world and we can send our thoughts to those who remain on Earth and are in need of prayer. We can also seek rebirth into a life that will help others. For the comparative few that have progressed high enough in their spiritual journey, they can become the Teachers and Guides whose whole existence is a spiritual one.

Spirit world contains every area we need to further our development. Everything we can think of can be manifested, attained and mastered in its energetic form. Yet there are restrictions; to attain the level where we have total freedom in the kind of heaven we build for ourselves, we must develop and we are limited and defined by what we have achieved to date. So if we are a very selfish person, we will be limited as to what we can manifest 'upstairs.' If we only think of ourselves, then we may only be able to create things for ourselves; we would not be able to interact and relate to the vastness of the energy around us, not as retribution, but because we have spent life thinking in an inward direction. If instead, we have spent our life thinking outwardly and seeing the bigger picture and acting upon it to help others, then we are prepared for what comes. It might still be a shock to arrive to any form of after-life, but the more our inner voice has been heeded in our physical life and we have lived a life in accordance with it, so it is easier for us to continue without the physical form attached. If by contrast, we have denied our inner-life, denied the spiritual and ignored our emotions in preference for our worldly and material ambitions, then the transition into the world of spirit will not only be a shock, we simply won't know how to relate to a world that is built for our soul, because we have ignored it for so long. Therefore, how far we can progress in Heaven can be directly limited to the extent we have prioritised material possessions and desires solely for their own sake.

The more we give freely down here and the more open our minds, then the more we are able to create and interact 'above' because we are thinking outwardly and with concern for others, which is the whole basis of a spiritual existence. So, if we pass over with a clear conscience and have lived peacefully, considering others alongside ourselves, our soul can soar free. This is another example of why we say we get back twice what we give out, because we receive the benefits of good feelings when we give of a clear conscience and the benefit of a clearer life in the world of spirit. So the more we have taken time to understand our own inner landscape, the more the geography of spirit world is accessible to us. Heaven can wait, but it is only denied us if we deprive our inner selves an outer existence.

An evolved spirit in spirit world lives in a world of pure consciousness and with no day or night to mark time, it is an ongoing existence. The absence of time means that there is no measure of existence. Just as we can sleep and have a very detailed dream in a short space of time, so up in spirit world, one thought or pastime can absorb us for what seems like a brief moment, but could be years in length, for there is no measure by which to judge. No day or night, no seasons, no imposed timetable or deadlines to meet and no need to sleep or to feed ourselves. We could spend decades up there between physical lives and yet it could feel like mere moments to our soul.

For a young soul, there may not be such a long gap between physical lifetimes. This is partly because a young soul will have a great need for experience and also because the younger the soul, generally speaking, the less detailed its requirements for learning and knowledge. Young souls need to experience a broad curriculum of life, while older souls may have very specific needs. This is because they have experienced life and learned from it, but will still need to address certain areas so that they may educate and elevate themselves in a particular way. They may for instance, want to learn how to heal and need to become a doctor or nurse or paramedic and it takes time to find that particular role for them. A younger soul by definition, has relatively little experience, so most situations will be new to it, therefore its needs are broad and can be met all the quicker.

The consciousness of a younger soul in spirit world will differ from that of an older soul in many ways. In a way, a younger soul is more elemental and basic and lacks a deep experience of itself in physical life. A younger soul has only limited ways of manifesting environments in spirit world, because its experience is less and its understanding is limited. It lacks the depth present in an older soul.

An older soul is in many ways more solid. It has had the learning time on Earth to develop a depth of experience, which creates its library of knowledge and it also has a deeper understanding of itself, which means it can manifest with more certainty as a body in spirit world. Just as in life, when we know ourselves we become more solid as people, so the experienced soul becomes more solid in spirit world. The key to understanding ourselves is to understand other people, for in so doing, we develop patience, flexibility and forgiveness. The older we get as a soul, the more opportunity we have to be wise and wisdom in the world of spirit can be defined as recognising how central love is to our existence.

We have touched upon how spirit world gives us places to learn, heal and build, but perhaps the most difficult aspect for us to comprehend is just how different our priorities are up there. Here on Earth, we need to look after our bodies, be concerned with day-to-day distractions and to cope with the demands of life. There, our only priority is that of the soul. The soul has an inner desire to better itself and experience. So, if our soul is desperate to help its fellow mankind, then it will seek out the best place to develop in spirit world. Such a soul might take itself to places of creativity to develop its artistic side, so that it can be ready to show others beauty through art. Alternatively, it might be naturally attracted to areas where scientific discovery is the focus. In so doing, it can absorb ideas that will drive it forward in its next life here on Earth. Come what may, on all but the seventh level, there will be a thirst and a need to manifest once more down on Earth. The learning each soul gains in spirit world can serve as the central driving force in the next life. Our priorities in spirit world are purely about our innermost needs and there is no interference from the distractions that can take priority here on Earth.

All those born with a wish to pursue one particular path and especially those pursuits which benefit others are invariably a calling that originated in spirit world. This calling will have been with us before we took our place in the womb. For others, we develop an interest in a particular area while we are down here and it is this then that grows as something we want to do, or a driving force we find we cannot ignore.

There are those born to physical life who possess a compelling drive to do one thing in their lives, not for themselves, but for those they can help, be it to become a research scientist, a conservationist championing the planet or a campaigner for the underprivileged. Each of us has an Earthly purpose and so, while for some seemingly unapparent reason people are born with this inner drive and purpose, invariably it is an expression of their soul's wish.

Quite often down here we can become confused as to what we should prioritise in our lives and especially if we have a giving nature, achieving a balance between meeting our personal needs and those of others can be problematic. This is where we learn to be true to ourselves. Once we know what we want to achieve and what our own limitations are, everything begins to fall into place all the more naturally. Being true to yourself, while maintaining a compassionate and spiritual outlook is an answer in itself, because it helps rid you of the doubts that might otherwise plague you.

If we are truly doing everything we can for ourselves and others for the right reasons, then we aren't going to be judged for making mistakes along the way out of our human foibles and ignorance. If we have a calling that will benefit others, it is all the more likely to be born of a spiritual nature. Such a calling provides us with a clarity of purpose that is unquestionable and it is when we fulfil it that our life becomes clear and full.

This is very different to when we are motivated to serve our own selfish ambitions with total disregard for others. These are two ends of a spectrum that only exists because of our own weaknesses. In a perfect world, we would all be motivated out of pure love for one another, however this is very far from where the human race exists right now. The very fact that we are here on Earth means we are all still 'at school', learning and growing while we find our pathway of progression.

Our motivation and our state of mind can be very closely linked. If we have a clear purpose and if that purpose is to help other people, then we have a clear conscience and with a clear conscience comes a greater clarity of thought. A clear mind and a clear conscience make us comfortable with ourselves and being comfortable with ourselves means the world is a much easier place to live in.

So it is, that there is a very real and direct link between how we experience life down here and our motivation. If we are motivated out of love, while life may still be hard, we are able to live with ourselves and have less regrets and confusion to clutter our brains. This is because we are clear that we are merely trying to do the best for other people that we can. This also means that when we pass over, we will know ourselves all the better and be more able to progress, unburdened by grudges, doubts and debts we need to repay.

This is one reason why so many spiritual traditions refer to us as creating our own world and why we are able to create heaven and hell by our actions. So, the clearer we are in ourselves, the clearer the geography of spirit world is to us and the more freedom we have to choose what we experience and where we go.

The life of your mind

Each soul is a complete individual that is part of a much wider universal whole. Whether we are on heaven or Earth, we never lose our distinct identity. Yet, a spiritual life calls upon us to consider all the billions of other souls that share life with us.

So it is, that when we choose to progress spiritually, there can be an inner dilemma between what we want, how fulfilled we feel and a resultant conflict between our heart and our head. The temptation, when we encounter problems that feel too big for us, is to ignore them, try to overcome them through sheer force of will, manipulate our way out of them or put the responsibility on someone else. A spiritual life is an invitation to take both personal responsibility and to recognise the equal importance of other people and ourselves. Therefore, this can make life seem tougher than if we were merely looking out for ourselves alone and did not consider the actual effects of our actions. It can seem easier to act selfishly than to seek fairness. Likewise we might want to blame others rather than recognise the role we ourselves play, when it is seemingly more convenient to get someone else to shoulder our burdens. A life of self-recognition demands that we look at life not solely for what we get from it, but how it can help us become stronger. By carrying our own load, being more honest, admitting our mistakes, respecting other people's choices and being as true to ourselves as we can be, we become more warm hearted and solid. By reflecting upon the consequences of what we do, we become more flexible and widen the choices on offer. By challenging ourselves and our opinions in this way, we can build a whole new picture of life in our minds.

One of the keys to progressing spiritually is understanding the validity of a having a spiritual element in our lives. At the very least we have to be sure there is at least the possibility of a bigger picture, of something existing outside the physical. If we have at least openness to belief, then we have the foundations for faith and faith can move mountains.

Your beliefs, your attitudes and your approach to life are key to your progression and the world of spirit will be behind you every time you take a positive step on your spiritual pathway. Therefore, a spiritual life is an opportunity to truly shape your destiny, not merely of who you are as a person, but what you receive and appreciate in life.

Whenever we say to ourselves 'I want to know more,' 'I want to experience more' then this opens a door for the universe. It doesn't mean we have to buy an airline ticket to realise our goal, but we can bring in new things that help us to discern what makes us truly happy. It may be as simple as watching the sun rise, a tree in the wind or the stars hanging in empty space in the night sky.

If you want to know more about life and yourself, you can achieve it by or performing a small act of kindness for someone in need. Bake some biscuits for your work colleagues on a Monday morning, or take the time to reflect on how you can improve the relationships in your life for the better and these small steps can help you develop your clarity of vision. Because one small act of good will can show us how quickly good feelings can come to us. Doing things for other people, sharing with good-will, can help us take our mind off of ourselves and if we do, we are on the right track. Small gestures are paving stones on our pathway to personal development but they also aid our progression. We do not develop solely by meditating; making the effort, becoming more flexible, being kind, thinking of other people, putting our own selfish thoughts aside are all essential elements of spirituality. This isn't a case of earning merit for being seen to do the right thing. If we change the way we are as a person for the better, not so we look good doing it, but to recognise that we feel good in making the effort, then it can help us recognise the goodness in ourselves and so, further our progression.

A life with purpose

In spirit world, we are in one sense, the embodiment of our thoughts. How we are is what we are. When we are at our very clearest, when we are free of all the burdens of physical existence, what remains is our spiritual form.

Up above are billions of souls and to better understand the journey we share with them, we can look at the example of a soul as it passes over and what experience it has as it joins with spirit world.

If we look at a person who has lived their life as mindfully as they are able and taken a spiritual perspective on board, still they may have regrets when their physical body dies. So at the time their soul ascends, they will feel the passing of all the aches and pains of physical life. The body falls away and they find themselves being drawn into the light above, experiencing their innermost self without the pain of living. Like awakening from a dream, they arrive to a pure beauty beyond words. They have flown upwards into Heaven and into a feeling of pure indescribable bliss that cannot be replicated on Earth. This soul will be in a place from whence they do not wish to return, where all the very best feelings are experienced, because they have come home to be at one with the spiritual universe. Angelic choirs, a vast spaciousness filled with love and the purest essence of life will envelop them. Once the crossing is complete, this soul will move onto the next stage and be called to account for the life they have lived. They will feel all of their life in one stream of consciousness, like watching a film of their existence before them, with all the attendant emotions. The beauty of life will be felt in recognising what they had on Earth, all the moments when it was the best it could be, alongside the pangs of conscience when they let others down.

As their life was a good one, there will be little to account for, yet still they will be shown those moments where selfishness won out over conscience and minor transgressions that are yet to be addressed. Because this soul cares for others, they will experience regret. This is part of the pull they will feel to be reborn and live a life that redresses the balance.

Of greatest importance by far is whether that soul has learned the lessons of the life to which they were last born. Perhaps they were born to learn the lessons of coping with difficult relationships. If they have worked their way through this curriculum of learning, choosing which relationships to nurture and recognising those which offered no hope of bonding and love, that soul will instantly feel they have achieved their goal. The next life will not hold similar challenges and it will be an opportunity for further progress. It may be that soul is perfectly placed to now care for others because they have learned to deal with their emotional pain without reacting negatively. So, this soul may now aspire to be a nurse or doctor, someone who can deal with the pain of others while they help them to heal.

By contrast, a soul which has passed over from a life of troublesome, unfulfilling, hurtful relationships that overwhelmed it, may still have more learning to do. Yet it can now relate to the pain of others in similar situations. So it may have a calling to become a psychiatrist or counsellor, or therapist when reborn, where its understanding can be applied, so that a life of negativity becomes fuel for helping those in whom it can relate to.

For nothing is ever wasted. Everything we go through brings us experience, providing us with the potential for growth. By doing something good, informed by a painful past, we can heal our wounds and create a better future for ourselves and, just as importantly, for everyone else too.

All of us are placed in life with a purpose and we are now, most definitely, in the right place at the right time for our progression.

A journey into spirit world

It is possible to elevate our minds so that we might access the wonder of the spiritual world which did we but know it, is part of our existence and our everyday lives. For above us is our truest home, that part of our universe where our soul resides and which endures beyond all else. We can learn to go there with our mind and find that which we might so easily otherwise forget or remain ignorant of. Join us in a journey into the world of spirit to experience yourself as you are in your freest most unencumbered form.

While we live here, we still have an allotted space in spirit world, so that our residence there is maintained in between lives. There you will find that of which you have most need, what is most appropriate to you and your understanding. For there are very many souls there who might educate and help us; more souls awaiting rebirth than have a physical existence down here. There dwell our Higher Selves and links to the souls of everyone who lives on Earth. For our soul, while we still live on the planet, maintains its spiritual connection to the everlasting source.

Embark with us on a journey to spirit world, to where our souls go when they leave our bodies and this Earthly habitat. To do so, we must rise upwards, so that we might join this realm of energy that resides on a separate plane, parallel to our own. Like journeying into space, we can mentally rise, higher and higher, leaving behind all the Earthly and familiar feelings of our bodies. Allowing our emotions to fall away, rising as if upon a celestial elevator, we ascend, feeling all that is Earthly fall below us as we rise into the ethereal levels. As we do, we become aware that around us are layers of colour, with a sensation of joy and freedom that is almost indescribably perfect. We allow all that is heavy and physical that serves to weigh us down to fall away. We feel the innermost part of our consciousness, untroubled by the afflictions of life, connecting with the spiritual source of all that we are. Here, is the feeling of familiarity that many of us do not even suspect exists and yet, the lack of which we can feel every day in our lives.

Emerging into a white bright light, we find firm floor beneath our feet, clouds and mist recede behind us and, as the haze clears, we see a valley faintly through the light. This valley is beautifully verdant and green, vibrantly alive with emerald colour and stretching on forever, bordered by small hills and fjords and rivers. The very air is so alive with the essence of life that it suffuses all of our consciousness and merely to be here is a source of perfect joy.

We feel the energy as it courses through every cell of our being alongside the oneness of finding ourselves connected with each and every atom of existence. All of our senses are wide open, so that the merest touch is felt in its total completeness and, all the while, the spacious clarity of our perception brings sight, smell and touch without interference. The lush grass beneath our feet is perfect in every way, dotted with golden buttercups that have a solidity and depth far beyond what we could imagine on Earth. The sky is blue and so deep that it seems to have a life of its own, dotted with white fluffy clouds that suspend themselves on invisible threads of energy, so near that you could almost touch them and so complete that it is wondrous to behold. It is almost beyond our comprehension to experience just how peaceful and safe we feel, to have this level of existence revealed without any threat of harm. There is only peace and safety here as we stand alone amongst a magnificence so perfect that as an observer, we wish only to join ourselves with it.

We ask to meet with those that dwell on this higher spiritual level. Before us appear beautiful souls; women, men and children. All coming forwards, just out of reach but visible so that we might recognise them for who they are and the state they have attained. Some are younger souls and some are older souls, some are dressed in older styles of clothing and some are more modern, for they have just arrived. Each of these souls is in their rightful place, living now amongst the beauty of an existence that is their reward for every good thing they have done in their lives. The very young who are loved for what they are and those who have lived longer and experienced more of life on Earth.

There are other planes or spheres up here and here we stand on a very good plane, while above us are those which stretch up higher and higher into seeming infinity. Here we are in a sphere where everyone is joined as one and united through a thought process that travels from one to another. In a naturally trusting unity of mutual camaraderie, information is shared and each soul learns from each other. They are all joined in a oneness that has no need of leaders or elders, for here is a uniformity of blessed existence that stretches to oblivion. Many souls congregate here, far more than our Earthly minds could ever hope to encompass with understanding. For here is a level of reality beyond our Earthly experience and with more souls inhabiting it than we could ever think possible, more souls than we can number, each with their own mind that, were we to dwell here in spiritual form, would be instantly known to us, just as we would be known to them.

Each soul has a place and a group to which they belong. Some toil and work hard at bettering themselves and endeavour to put right the wrongs that they committed in Earthly life and the actions they committed out of ignorance. Some, those who wish to share, create experiences for others, gardens and landscaped natural environments that are fashioned from pure thought, so that the effort involved requires them to express their will with focus, as they recall what shape these objects held in their Earthly habitat. Some build spiritual places that are an expression of their wish to venerate all that is good in the universe and bring to others this same depth of feeling.

While the nature of this work is difficult for us to understand, each soul on this level is constructing something of positive benefit for others. If they build a place of worship, when that soul returns to

Earth in its next life, it will wish to bring spirituality into its life, because that is its highest aspiration.

There are many types of endeavour, there are amongst these souls, those who save souls that have just come over to spirit world, while some are focused on providing tuition, running schools for those that wish to advance themselves and learn. Some hold the form of a previous life and some change their form to that which they held in a life they adored. There are many different varieties of people here, all races, creeds and colours and yet there is no distinction, for everyone is on an equal plane and all are one.

All know of God and each of them are aware of the Higher Levels and wish to progress, to advance themselves and become that which they have not yet fully realised. They wish to succeed on their journey so they might grow and manifest as a soul even more complete in its beauty. Each one has a place they call home and that place is magnificent. They have dwellings and they have rivers, oceans, mountains, trees and flowers. Every element is a manifestation of the soul that has created it. Each one has that which they enjoy.

There are dwellings for the children, villages full of the young who are alive with life, bubbly, full of enthusiasm and playful happiness. They are playing and laughing and learning to interact with one another. Amongst them are older souls, women and men who care for them and they are so happy you can feel the euphoria that emanates from each and every one. It is a place of promise, joy, and delight, where the laughter brings with it hope for the future of these children. For their turn will come to be introduced to this man-made world and life will take on new meaning. Then, they will have everything that they learn from where they are now in spirit world. Some will grow into mature people before they are sent down and some will start as young-minded souls full of promise.

So we have young souls and old souls that will be prepared to come down and grow here on the Earth and bear their own children. Here in spirit world, there is no pain, no spite, no jealousy, just loving souls who are happy with each other. Acceptance, bonding and unconditional love shine and radiate from this plane in their purest form, unsullied by care and worry, and there are no negativities to intrude upon this level of existence.

Elsewhere, there are souls pursuing all the areas of interest and endeavour that they wish to bring to life, to themselves and to fruition. For in spirit world, we can further the interests that consumed us in life and those that we were unable to engage in and we wish to continue, so they will be part of the driving force in our next rebirth.

Here are all forms of pursuit and the souls are working really hard, because they are committed for one reason or another. So we see them drawing as architects, creating music and filling the sky with sound, building bridges and boats and doing what they have always wanted.

All are either continuing on a job they have not finished from when they were once down here on Earth, or furthering themselves by taking an interest in things they have not yet achieved. They toil and they think and they plan very hard.

Some are giving their best for mankind down here, so that their thoughts may be communicated, transferred from spirit world, for us on the Earth plane to receive. There are gardeners who are growing magnificent gardens with flowers, trees, beautiful parks and animals that run wild.

This is a place that is imbued with beauty and is wonderful to see. Souls live here in freedom and the joy of being alive, living and doing the things they so desperately wanted to do when they were on this Earth plane and perhaps did not have the chance or the

181

confidence to make it happen. Yet, here they are fulfilling their dreams and desires expressing themselves and living out that for which they hoped and wanted.

This is a place of love, the love of their work, the love of what they are doing. Each soul is bringing into being that which they wish for and that which they are entitled to. So, there are blacksmiths, mechanics and engineers, people who build railways, trains, aeroplanes, and cars. There are builders, draughtsmen and all those who would bring something to this Earth. Artists, musicians, creative people of all kinds, potters, sculptors; they are all here making their art and their work succeed so that they might fulfil their dreams.

There are also many places of healing in spirit world, hospitals which take the wounded, the ones that have suffered greatly emotionally and physically in physical life, both the young and the old. Everyone is tended to and looked after, in a place where they might grow and gain strength and release themselves from the pain they experienced when they were down here on the Earth. For pain lingers within the soul and it needs the passage of time to rest and heal, before it might move on from its suffering. For those who have died in shock, the soul needs time to adjust, to heal itself and to become aware of where it is now, in the heaven that soul has created for itself. For in spirit world, we may only experience that which we can comprehend and we can only embody that which we have earned.

Those souls who are in need of care are nurtured and nursed by the very best, with love, patience and compassion. Both adult souls and children may join this place; all are looked after and are very special.

In all levels of our experience, in all our lives, both the physical and the spiritual, we all have a place and a purpose, both in where we are and where we are destined to journey. Our life on this Earth plane can be joyous if we wish it to be. Yet we all receive emotional and physical pain and this can make its mark, for even if our challenges do not serve to make us negative, still we carry the burden of having faced them. For until we are fully liberated, in both our hearts and our minds through a spiritual awakening, our wounds can remain as scars and the weight we have born can leave us weakened, pessimistic or in denial that something better might await us.

Spirit world is not where we end our lives, or escape to, it is a continuation of life where God looks after us, protects us and keeps us safe. The world we create there is one where all the very best we are able to enjoy and to aspire to is created in the image of what we know. For the forms, the buildings, the landscapes and the natural beauty in spirit world are all created from what we know of the physical world. All these things originate on Earth and it is our recollection of them that enables us to recreate. So we may have parks and gardens and lakes and rivers, all created from what we know from life. God has enabled the environments in which we might independently grow, so that we might create the very best of what we know.

So spirit world is a beautiful place and our thoughts once we are there focus on the living down here on the Earth plane, the ones we grew with and loved, the ones we interacted with at work and at play. We think of them as we hope they think of us. On the other side, if we feel someone on the Earth plane has a special thought for us, then our heart will fill with love. For we grow and fulfil our place in heaven when we are loved from both worlds. So it is up to us to bring this love and good will with us when we pass over. Every part and every thought we have is taken over to the other side when we pass. For we have a purpose there and a place to go. The roles we play, who we are, what we say and what we do is all part of us when we arrive there. We are what we are and it is what we are that we wish to improve; to do good and to give out goodwill, love, peace and harmony to everyone. It is so easy to do so when you are on the other side in spirit world. But if you have a sad heart because you have done wrong when down here, then you will want to make amends, you will want to redress the balance and to make things better. You will want to come down and ask for forgiveness or bring your sorrow as shame, for these feelings weigh very heavily upon you on the other side in spirit world. You are accountable for your actions and so you are called upon to make amends for those deeds which harmed others.

For if we have wronged many or one, it is up to each of us to attempt to repair the damage we have caused. So, if we have lived a life of deliberate harm, our hearts can weigh very heavy when we arrive at this wonderful place, for our deeds in life will preclude us from entering. Badness may not enter a high level in spirit world and you cannot gain entry if you are not worthy of it.

When we pass over, all we want to do is arrive at this place. Like looking through the gates into a glorious garden, we will naturally want to gain entry. The only thing that can hold us outside is our awareness of our own shortcomings and who we are. Like a magnetic field, we are rejected by that which is opposite and the price of entry is a life well lived.

For our self-justification is merely that and the only thing we might do is to fully confront who and what we are. So we learn the error of our ways and we do it the hard way if we leave it too late. If you are in this situation where errors need to be rectified, you will want to come down here to Earth to make amends. If you have caused emotional harm, you will want to come and make a special place down here for those who are around you and are loving you. Yet to improve this physical world is not easy, for there are too many individuals and too many groups of people learning their own rules that are at odds with love.

Each life gives us a chance. Each time we come, we can repair the damage and, we can make amends for ourselves and everyone, so that we may reach the place we call Heaven and live under God's eyes, under God's wing, under God's Law and know that we are special. For we are the children of God, we belong to him and our Earthly lives are part of that Creation. We have parents here that give us this Earthly body through which the soul may join and, working as a team, we might achieve great things. But if you separate yourself and do not do the things that the soul wishes for you, then your inner-self, your reasoning, your common sense, your love is being denied and you will slow your journey. For love is what is meant for the world and for each other and by treating ourselves and others kindly we realise our journey.

Chapter Twelve - Angels

Angels function to help the human race and are direct agents of God who exist to express and further His will. The way in which they are born is the same as the way in which our souls are born, birthed from God according to His plan. So an angel is born as are we, into spirit world, into a world of energy as a being of divine energy and exists to help human souls while they are in their physical bodies. Theirs is a pathway of learning and knowledge, of growing to help our souls as we meet the demands of our existence.

This role fulfils the angel's divine journey and enables them to mature. Yet, when they have gained enough experience, all angels reach a point where they have a choice, they can either continue to pursue their divine spiritual life, or they can choose to continue their journey by entering the form of a human soul. At this point of decision, an angel may either progress as a teacher of the younger angels, passing on its knowledge and experience, or it may move on and gain even deeper experience of the human condition, by moving on and taking human form.

Those angels that choose to come down here and experience physical life have a very hard beginning. They will need to enter a new phase of existence, moving from their spiritual form into that of a human being and because they are perfect beings, this birth into a human body is a shock. The impact of finding their consciousness in an imperfect body in an imperfect world is like being ripped from one reality and placed in another. All their being will, up until that point, have been experienced purely in God's realm and then they emerge into a physical existence, with another form around them. This is like the shock of drowning, when no longer are you able to draw sustenance from the reality around you. For an angel is used to being whole in its celestial existence, where everything is pure and once they have joined us on the road of physical existence, they are subject to all the emotional and material influences of this world that we contend with and enjoy. Therefore, like us, once here, some angels can be subject to internal battles to submit to temptation, but their background dictates that their true pathway is one of goodness.

The initial shock of arrival, therefore, is too much for an angel to safely bear and survive, they will need a way of experiencing the human form without being thrust into a full human life. So, an angel, when it first arrives in a human womb will typically arrive into the body of a baby that is destined not to live. So, an angel will first join with a foetus destined to miscarry, terminate, or be born for just a few days' existence before it passes over. This arrival educates the angel to the nature of life and physical pain, for up until now they would only be familiar with the emotional pain of human beings. It also prepares the angel for the experience of arriving into a physical body, a far greater shock for a mature spiritual being such as an angel, than it is for a human soul.

Angels are not the cause of a termination or a miscarriage, they can see the outcome of that pregnancy and join with it at the time when the human foetus is developed enough to receive them. So, a baby's life is not then taken in vain, but that pregnancy has helped an angel to take human birth and to learn of human existence and then to return to the human community in spirit world, where it can congregate with family members and gain direct experience of what it is to be human, before it is ready to truly arrive in its next life here on Earth.

In our age, angels arrive because there is so much pain in the world, we need them to come and bring their wisdom to us. However, an angel that wishes to continue its journey as a human, because it is attuned to the pain of the world, will be sensitive and liable to pick up on humanity's pain. After enough experience in human suffering, an angel will then be ready, learning quickly how it may bring its wishes for progression into the world. An angel is like an agent that wants to find and increase the goodness in life. They see the good in those around them, wish to bring happiness and peace into human existence, while being sensitive and saddened by the unnecessary pain they see around them. If we were to look at the world through the eyes of an angel we would cry too, for the level of their wisdom allows them to see life for what it is and to perceive the full folly of much of what we do. At the same time, they are a force for pure good and when they emerge amongst us, as the golden children that they are, humanity is all the better for it.

Now, as once before, we have angels arriving amongst us to help the human race steer its course, for many of us are lost and seeking a direction that will bring peace to the face of the Earth.

How do we find God?
God is already part of our lives and the real question is not how we find Him, but rather how we recognise His presence and then allow it into our lives. Life is already a spiritual journey and finding the spiritual meaning within it is a stepping-stone, allowing us to recognise that there is purpose in every moment. Finding this purpose is, in turn, a stepping-stone to recognising that, like every part of our existence, there is an originating Thought and that His is the ultimate purpose. So, we find God by opening our minds to what is going on in life. Recognising the beauty and splendour of life, observing the flow of the natural world while appreciating what it is we have shows us that there is so much more on offer. There are limitless possibilities and limitless rewards we can find on our journey and these are things we find both for ourselves and within ourselves. For in finding God, we are going beyond our connection with existence and finding our connection with its ultimate meaning. Once we find that there is no beginning and no end to life, that we can create today what we wish to bring into the world and that we are the originators of our own experience, we can see that there is a wider purpose and that which holds true for us, holds true for the entirety of existence. So, what we might otherwise take to be random events, can be seen for what they are, the natural consequence of the underlying spiritual nature of the world we live

in.   This helps us also to differentiate between what troubles so many, which is why pain coexists with splendour and hope. For, it is beauty we are born into and it is our choice as human beings as to what we make of it, whether we add to the woes of the world or whether we are prepared to take a pathway of progression that enhances ourselves and the world around us.

If we adjust our view of the world to recognise that is a spiritual home for us all, we can see that by giving out what we would want back, we are feeding ourselves and those around us. Adopting this approach can be the result of having a conscience, while at the same time, this attitude creates greater conscience within us. For giving feeds us within.

If we are able to accept that there are those who are less fortunate than us and that we are all here to help each other, we can see the correlation with the role God plays with us. This can add to our understanding of ultimate love and how God would want the best for each and every one of us, no matter who we are. We can then understand why He would treat all of us as equal, for in His eyes, we are. What stands in the way of putting our conscience first is our selfishness, our ignorance of the way things truly are and our pride and specifically the pride that tells us there is nothing capable of being greater than ourselves. If we are able to progress beyond these internal hindrances, there is a much bigger world waiting for us, both here and above. For the more we are able to accept and welcome a greater understanding into our own lives, the more we are able to receive on the other side, both now and when we pass from this particular life of experiences.

Here on Earth, we need to go through a journey to recognise the spiritual nature of life. On the other side, it is there around us and we are part of it. Just this simple recognition is one of the most liberating things we can bring to our lives, because within each of us is the ability to be part of the most wonderful spiritual playground of existence that is as real as the air we are breathing and can nurture every element of our beings if we choose to draw upon it.

Turn within yourself and imagine what it would be like if all your negativities and regrets were not there. When we pass over into God's realm, the first thing we encounter will be how we feel about ourselves. Knowing this, we have the chance to put things right and to fill our lives with the cause for happy memories, right now, while we have this golden opportunity.

Change

You are what you are, regardless of the things you have done and also because of them. This means that every day you awaken, you have a chance to be the person you would want to be.

The desire for expansion is a search for personal freedom and clarity and the growth that comes with it can be painful, because whenever we desire to change, to achieve it, we have to learn to be without something that was previously part of our lives.

When we are looking for a life that is more suited to who we are, we may have to put aside our judgement of ourselves or other people, to remove harmful things or thoughts from our life, to rid our self of mental obstructions, or to face the prospect of removing ourselves from harmful situations. So whatever it is we are looking to be, we can only be that by putting aside that which we would rather we were not. When we arrive at our destination, we may find that we have not actually travelled very far, but what we have gained on that journey is an inner wisdom born of insight. Finding God is not a physical journey, it is an extension of our spiritual journey that demands we consider the ultimate purpose of life. The search for this ultimate meaning gives us the opportunity to tie up our loose ends and weave the pattern of life that suits our soul.

The geography of spirit world

To say that spirit world has a geography is misleading, it is a world of energy and much of what exists there is created from our own minds. But because our minds relate to a spatial existence, we need a way of understanding how each area there exists in relation to all those around, above and below them.

The first thing to understand is that spirit world is created by God and is His home. So it is His thought that has created the environment in which our souls live. In the same way, to the extent that we are able, when we pass over we are able to create our own environments within spirit world.

At the highest levels, while it is a world of energy with a divine dream like quality to it, we relate to spirit world as if it is a physical place, with physical centres but that is because that is how our human minds are configured to relate to any external reality. So when we talk of any 'place' over there, it is not a physical location, but the structure of reality in an environment of purest energy.

There, we can walk on grass, touch walls of marble, meet other souls, but it is not as physically real as being on Earth, rather it is like being in the most lucid dream imaginable, where the only limitation is us. So, we can build houses and create great works of art, but the most important aspect is our ability to be real ourselves and we achieve this by becoming beings that are spiritual in nature. So, the wider our minds, the clearer our consciences, the further we have progressed and the wider our minds, the greater our ability to create will be on the other side.

While spirit world is like a physical reality, we do not have physical restrictions. If we are able, we can maintain a human form over there and walk and talk as if we are on Earth, but we do not see or speak, we do not propel ourselves through the action of our physical body and our speech is, in reality, the communication of our soul energy.

While the contours of our mind give our thoughts a physical shape in life, the continuation of our eternal existence is remembered by our soul and not by our brain. So when we return to Earth, we will not remember spirit world, but our soul will retain a sense of longing for an existence that is pure and unencumbered by the restraints of human life, just as is in spirit world, almost all of us will long for the impact of physical reality. This seeming contradiction is what creates the human condition. Here on Earth we feel the longing of our soul, there in spirit world we might still be attached to the things that are only available to us in physical life. For over there, such pursuits as drinking and eating are mere shadows of the real thing. We can remember what a cool drink feels like, but we cannot experience it directly, only bring the manifestation of it into our world, where it would be very like the real thing, but because we have no real thirst over there, we cannot feel true refreshment. We cannot feel full or hungry, cannot eat a chocolate or a wholesome meal. There we cannot have physical consummation in any of its forms, and in love it is the emotional aspect we experience. In spirit world we have the ability to join with another soul, to share without loss, to give without limitation and to experience the purest of joys. Yet, we may wish to communicate with those we loved in life and treasured, such as our partners, children, wider family and friends.

The higher levels in spirit world are attained only once we are able to give up our attachment to Earthly pleasures, not because these pleasures are repugnant or bad, but because we have recognised there is greater fulfilment to be had from the blissful feelings that accompany a spiritual existence. That does not mean we need to live the life of a religious devotee to progress, or even that we must follow a religious pathway. Rather, we are called upon to look beyond the short-term and identify where our inner feelings of fulfilment originate from. In so doing, we can recognise what is most important to us and live our life with an enhanced level of self-awareness. For progression is as much about what we are willing to leave behind because it has served its purpose, as much as it is about seeking out what will serve us best.

To travel, to experience and to find our way in spirit world is far less hazardous than it is on Earth. There, we have no disease, no suffering, no famine, no war and no natural disasters. To get to a place, we merely need to imagine it and we are there. Likewise, if we wished to travel by walking or cycling, we can imagine ourselves doing so and it would happen. We can look at events on Earth and be near to our loved ones, witnessing their slower Earthly progress and send our good thoughts and feelings to them, in the same way that we can hear them as they think of us or send their good wishes. So in many ways, spirit world is the playground of our soul, but to live there, we have to learn to give up the body and everything that is physical and materialistic, while we retain the memory of all our actions of life on Earth.

God sits at the head of everything, above all, and below are the angels, guides, teachers, and then the seven layers of human spiritual existence, below which is the Earth. Penetrating through the middle of all these levels is our direct pathway to God, where we can communicate with him through our thoughts. This direct pathway is what we travel upwards and downwards upon our spiral of rebirth and learning. What we have done and how we have lived our life dictates which level we arrive at and dwell in between lives. Level seven, or sphere seven, is the ultimate level we can attain while remaining in human physical form and anything above this is a point of no return for our souls, where we can choose to stay in the spiritual dimension if we wish. Below level two we will have a hard time elevating ourselves. So all the levels between these two are where we will find the majority of humanity and the higher we go, the fewer souls we find and the more choices we have.

Within each level, there is a layout or geography. There are places we can travel to where our souls congregate and meet. There are entry points to receive those souls who have passed over and many places with a specific purpose, such as healing and learning and socialising. Each of these places has a purpose. In addition, we can create our own oases, places that are made by our mind for us to live in. These little bits of heaven are moulded by our behaviour on Earth. The higher we go, the more idyllic these homes for our soul can be. They are places where we can experience the perfection of what we have achieved. So the nature of our soul's spiritual sanctuary is both a consequence of the effort we have put into our life journey, as well as the ultimate we can currently obtain. The higher we go, the more comfortable and idyllic these dwelling places can be, because we experience them more completely. Here we can both express and find the most fulfilling elements of our nature. We find fulfilment that life did not allow us to pursue because of the priorities we had that stood in the way and we can pursue those interests we developed and perhaps excelled at in life. So for some, these personal havens will be beautiful gardens, for others they will be places to experience what we missed out on in physical life, a continuation of our desire to be creative, to learn the sciences or to live in harmony with the natural world. Of course we are not restricted to these areas. If we wish, we can go out and pursue our journey in spirit world too. We can find the like-minded souls who dwell on our level and we can find natural outlets for our wish to help others on that plane, be it through teaching, learning, sharing, developing, or creating.

From level three and above we have increasingly more choice as to how to live in spirit world, up until level seven, where we are able to create our own permanent reality in which to dwell. So, for the purpose of exploring a level in spirit world, we are going to take a look at the higher levels, where the choices are that much more open for us.

The places of healing
Healing could almost be described as the purpose of our spiritual journey. On the highest levels we will find souls congregating in specific locations to be a part of healing all manner of life. There, in this spiritual reality, the healing to be found is of the highest order. Like entering a university or hospital dedicated to one specific purpose, these healing locations have many specific areas within

them. There will be departments for very spiritual forms of healing, where the souls gathered there will direct themselves to radiating love to the world, or influencing specific areas of healing of which the world is very much in need. There, very progressed souls will concern themselves with radiating peace to war-torn areas, sending love to those who have suffered the terrible emotional traumas that the vestiges of physical conflict and violence brings. They will radiate love to those who are suffering starvation, bringing solace and warmth to those who are bereft and directing purpose to those who may help the situation by bringing aid. The nature of this healing is to influence whole areas; to introduce ideas to all those who are suited to aiding positive spiritual purpose through their physical efforts. So, wherever there is the greatest need, they will bring the specific thoughts of healing that will be of most benefit.

If we were to approach these areas in spirit world, we would feel the immensity of purpose that manifests as energy radiating outwards like a corona of light and rays that penetrate outwards to our physical reality. It would be like seeing the aurora borealis in the night sky as the many waves and frequencies of heartfelt intention are emitted into the ether.

These souls are born for this purpose and on the highest levels, their whole reason for being is to provide healing where it is most needed and in the area they specialise. The location on level seven where this is expressed at its highest level is the equivalent of a nuclear reactor. There, the healing is carried out on such a high level that it penetrates all of human existence and beyond. The healers who live there are amongst the very highest of human souls and they exist only in this healing centre. The energy they radiate is so intense and it vibrates on such a frequency that it penetrates every level of reality, but here on Earth, it will not dictate the course of our actions, because our free will is the prerogative. So, this healing will have its most profound effect where there is the greatest need and the greatest opportunity for it to be experienced.

However we receive it, it is a force for good and it will manifest as a desire to help, as reassurance, enhancing our ability to move on from what it is that afflict us and to give us hope. If we are not ready for it and mentally tune into this area, the power that is emitted is so strong and so spiritual in nature, that it is akin to looking directly into the sun. Without the spiritual assistance that the places of healing provide, our world would be a very different place.

Each of us has the capacity to heal, both ourselves and others and our gift is enhanced by the presence of these healers that dedicate their beings to radiating healing throughout reality. They are the nucleus of healing and deal with the bigger picture of life. To reach this level and become one of these healers, we would have to go through many levels of experience, being a healer in our lifetime, being a healer in spirit world, accepting healing as the main course of our pathway, until it becomes the entire rationale for our soul.

Right now at this time, the human race is going through a particularly daunting time and it is very important that there are enough souls in spirit world who have the skills necessary to help us in the trials that face us in the future. Healing is perhaps the most important part of what will be needed in the years ahead. Therefore, an increasing number of us are questioning, seeking, recognising and becoming aware of the seemingly unexplainable spiritual elements of existence, to pave the way to meet this need.

Some of those that are exploring in this way will choose spirituality to be part of their life, healing and helping others here in our physical lives. The more of us that choose these pathways, then in the fullness of time, once they have passed over, there will be more souls in spirit world who can choose healing as their purpose and pursue a purpose of helping humanity in all its myriad forms.

On the highest levels, healers exist who work in unison with the angels. Like officers in an army, the angels each have their area of focus and human souls can work with them to bring their unique healing energies to bear in a concerted effort.

Alongside those who wish to heal the world, there are also those who concentrate on smaller areas of human need. Each level has its equivalent of the ultimate healing centre and the higher we ascend, the more profound this healing becomes.

So, on every level, we will find those souls that dedicate themselves to healing particular types of human problems, specialising in reaching out to the less fortunate who cannot help themselves. There are those that reach out to the sufferers of long term disease and disability, those who reach out to the blind and those who are emotionally bereft. In these areas, they will work on an individual basis and the focus of the healing is not necessarily to help our physical condition, but rather to aid us emotionally. Spiritual healers can work best with those who are open to helping themselves and are able to recognise that their trials can help others who are facing the same challenges in their existence.

The nature of spiritual healing is to work with energy, which can heal us emotionally and which may then allow our physical condition to improve, not least because this kind of healing can aid our ability to cope. Like a radio receiver, the effect of this healing from spirit world is greatly increased when we are willing to tune ourselves into it. If we accept that we cannot change reality, but that we can find purpose within it, then our lives are enhanced on many levels and that in itself helps us find meaning. Therefore, an openness to healing also enables us to change our focus and opens to us the same choices that the dedicated souls in spirit world have acted upon, which is to do what they can, whenever they can, to help those in need, despite their own limitations.

If we are a healer in spirit world, we might choose to dwell entirely in a centre of healing. We can also specialise in any one of numerous forms of healing. We can become an emotional counsellor and help those souls who have recently passed over, whatever their circumstances, we can tune into humanity or learn healing as a student, so that we might bring it into our next life on Earth. We can also learn to be a spiritual healer that helps spiritual healers on Earth, so when they heal others, they might tune into the healing energies we are in turn using.

So in spirit world, if that is the journey we have chosen for ourselves, we can be on any number of healing roads and we would gravitate to the healing centres on our level as the natural place to be.

The healing centres, on whatever level we find them, are effecting change for the better for all of humanity.

In spirit world, we tend to choose a form we are familiar with and presents ourselves at our best, so many people who passed over in old age will choose to manifest in their twenties or thirties. Nonetheless, in spirit world we naturally feel younger because all our physical aches and pains disappear along with our worldly concerns. However, when we project our physical forms to communicate with the living, we will put forward our image at the age our loved ones are familiar with. So a grandfather may appear at the most recent age we remember him, even though in spirit world he is enjoying the complete absence of age, sickness, disease and worry and his only concern is for those loved ones who remain on Earth.

The exception is those who passed over when they were still children. In this case, the spiritual form of that child will still need to grow and develop. Their needs will be taken care of by those who have dedicated themselves to this purpose.

Chapter Thirteen - The Progression

However we relate to God, whatever name we call Him by, or whether we merely realise that there is a supreme consciousness that exists in the Universe, it is our connection with Him that is of true importance. We may call him our Father or any other name that recognises His position and how He relates to us as Creator.

For, in reality, each of us possess only the tiniest fragment of His capacity and that is why we do not have the ability to comprehend His thought patterns or how He expresses His will. God is each moment of time for eternity and He is everything, everything that is and everything that was. He is the beginning and the infinite 'always.' His knowledge and understanding is greater than we could possibly comprehend or even touch upon. When visiting, He presents himself in a way we can relate to, for we cannot expand ourselves to comprehend Him, therefore He must project a form we can understand. He divides and multiplies constantly. All that is here on Earth and that which exists in Heaven, infinite landscapes of beauty, flora and fauna of every description is that which He has made and given to humanity. In Heaven the beauty is incorruptible, while here on Earth we can spoil that which has been given unto us as a magnificent gift. While we live in the Garden of Eden, it has become contaminated by the effects of our presence and our works.

What is it that God asks of us? Our human life is so short and yet this is why we have so many chances to be reborn. He gives us life, a world, forests, trees, sky, sun and food to feed and nurture us. Animals abound, to see and love and share on this planet of ours and yet we are so primitive.

It is inevitable that the Earth will end, but not through an act of mankind, rather through a process of the universe. Time stands still for God, but not for us and His planet has billions of years yet to live.

Before the planet Earth comes to an end and we progress on the next step of our spiritual journey, all religions shall come into one. There is a gateway on the other side in His realms that He has created for us. It is a gateway beside God that allows us to move on to the next spiritual realm, a level where we may permanently take our place in the spiritual universe. All of us are travelling towards this gateway, spiralling upwards towards spiritual goals, achieving enlightenment so that we might progress. That is why life is short, so that we might have our opportunities to learn myriad lessons, lessons that change with each of the situations we are born into. Some of us are striving to learn and consciously reach certain goals. Others are far more primitive and have a lot of learning before us.

The Day of Reckoning will be soon upon us, when each of us recognises that God exists, when He will answer our prayers and make Himself known. Many will recognise that the Kingdom of Heaven can be theirs.

A leader will come and will be the pathway and the gateway of understanding and his voice will be heard. For he comes with the knowledge and the understanding of what God portrays and what God has shown him. God's place is to watch and look after His flock and each individual person has the right to graze where they choose, but He will not let them stray too far. Our conscious thoughts will awaken to Him and to what He gives and brings to the children of this Earth. Some will accept readily and some will ponder and think and some will deny Him, but all will have been told. A rude awakening comes when we come in to His kingdom, the place we named Heaven, or God's home. As we as individuals divide and conquer, so will He. He does not conquer with brute force, rather He comes with love and spiritual awakening. There are many helpers here on this Earth and He has many voice-boxes who will speak from Him and for Him and they will all speak a common language that gathers people to them, for these voice-boxes all speak His words and speak for Him and they are all the same. So,

God will be heard and God will be answered through our actions, by those who choose to recognise His existence and those who choose to deny Him and their own inner knowledge. So, there will be wailing and crying and there will be prayers, for when His name is heard, it will be in the manner of a knowing, an inner recognition that we all share, whether we choose to recognise it or not. Individually, we will be aware of a spiritual call to awaken us to an existence beyond our own thoughts. All enlightened minds will share this understanding and each and every one will find their individual pathway according to their choice, knowing that there is a purpose to life. Some, who are afraid of change and not ready to neither adjust nor accept, God will lose them to barren land. In not pursuing His call, their growth will be stunted, while others who listen will find fertile ground for their progression.

For those who accept, God will give them inner direction and purpose. They will flourish and grow in harmony and splendour as they recognise the true meaning of life's gift and appreciate the feeling of God's love. To them will come an understanding, recognising the true meaning of who they are and that they will never again feel totally alone. God knows each of us personally and will reach out to us individually, subtly, over time, through our awareness and helping us relate to what feels right. Each will have their opportunity.

Unobtrusive and humble, God asks His children to accept His words, to trust them and love Him as God loves us. We have many, many, miles to go and there are innumerable pathways that all lead the pool of humanity to His word. Some will stand and fight and resist the following of God's leadership and those who fight will destroy and burn, believing that they are right and having the power of control. Angels will come and help the innocent, the children and the lambs of this world and lead them forward, to where all minds will be joined and new beginnings will come once more. A humble existence, where there is no forceful gain, one in which they share and are thankful for where they are, basking in the peace of mind that comes with their recognition. Each and every one, of different races, all equal in His eyes and all equal with each other. Violence will be feared and purity will reign. Purity of mind, purity of thought and the willingness to give and support.

Heaven is a place that God calls home and our home is a place that God calls learning, God gives us all the fruits and the tastes and the opportunities to grow. All He asks is that we love one another and love Him in return. For, He has created a place we call home. He has thought of us and offered us all the comforts He can give, all the fruits of this world and yet, it goes to the most part unnoticed. He has not lost sight of us as individuals, has not stopped listening to the cries from our hearts, but not all can be answered. We come to learn and our learning must be fulfilled, so intervening will delay and hold us back from our development. God is pleased with others who have been seen to struggle and strive and they have done Him proud. God sees everything from afar; our life is in His hands. For He can crush in a thought and take back in a moment but that is not His will, for it would undo everything we have strived for and we are nowhere near the end.

Times are better for some but for others are worse. There is no balance to be found, suffering is all over the World and that is why God asks that we be patient and learn and strive for beauty and splendour. Take time to stand in awe of the colours of life and the goodness that some people share, and we will learn far quicker than if we do nothing. His Life is law, it lasts forever and our world is short. So, make the most of the moment you have and the life that has been granted. For each of us is an individual and each soul unique to itself. God will embrace you and love you all the more when you return home.

For more information on our work, please visit
www.carolannspathway.co.uk
or email info@carolannspathway.co.uk

4799877R00120

Printed in Germany
by Amazon Distribution
GmbH, Leipzig